LOST CIVILIZATIONS

THE MINOANS

Don Nardo

LUCENT
BOOKS®

THOMSON

★

GALE

San Diego • Detroit • New York • San Francisco • Cleveland
New Haven, Conn. • Waterville, Maine • London • Munich

LIBRARY

THOMSON
———————✳———————™
GALE

© 2005 by Lucent Books. Lucent Books is an imprint of The Gale Group, Inc.,
a division of Thomson Learning, Inc.

Lucent Books® and Thomson Learning™ are trademarks used herein under license.

For more information, contact
Lucent Books
27500 Drake Rd.
Farmington Hills, MI 48331-3535
Or you can visit our Internet site at http://www.gale.com

LIBRARY OF CONGRESS CATALOGING-IN-PUBLICATION DATA

Nardo, Don, 1947–
    The Minoans / by Don Nardo.
    p. cm. — (Lost civilizations)
    Summary: Discusses the Minoans, their economy, government, social structure,
and art and architecture.
    Includes bibliographical references and index.
    ISBN 1-59018-565-X (hard cover : alk. paper)
  1. Minoans—Juvenile literature. I. Title. II. Series.
  DF220.3.N37 2005
  939'.1801—dc22
                                         2004010758

Printed in the United States of America

CONTENTS

FOREWORD

"What marvel is this?" asked the noted eighteenth-century German poet and philosopher, Friedrich Schiller. "O earth . . . what is your lap sending forth? Is there life in the deeps as well? A race yet unknown hiding under the lava?" The "marvel" that excited Schiller was the discovery, in the early 1700s, of two entire ancient Roman cities buried beneath over sixty feet of hardened volcanic ash and lava near the modern city of Naples, on Italy's western coast. "Ancient Pompeii is found again!" Schiller joyfully exclaimed. "And the city of Hercules rises!"

People had known about the existence of long lost civilizations before Schiller's day, of course. Stonehenge, a circle of huge, very ancient stones had stood, silent and mysterious, on a plain in Britain as long as people could remember. And the ruins of temples and other structures erected by the ancient inhabitants of Egypt, Palestine, Greece, and Rome had for untold centuries sprawled in magnificent profusion throughout the Mediterranean world. But when, why, and how were these monuments built? And what were the exact histories and beliefs of the peoples who built them? A few scattered surviving ancient literary texts had provided some partial answers to some of these questions. But not until Pompeii and Herculaneum started to emerge from the ashes did the modern world begin to study and re-

construct lost civilizations in a systematic manner.

Even then, the process was at first slow and uncertain. Pompeii, a bustling, prosperous town of some twenty thousand inhabitants, and the smaller Herculaneum met their doom on August 24, A.D. 79, when the nearby volcano, Mt. Vesuvius, blew its top and literally erased them from the map. For nearly seventeen centuries, their contents, preserved in a massive cocoon of volcanic debris, rested undisturbed. Not until the early eighteenth century did people begin raising statues and other artifacts from the buried cities; and at first this was done in a haphazard, unscientific manner. The diggers, who were seeking art treasures to adorn their gardens and mansions, gave no thought to the historical value of the finds. The sad fact was that at the time no trained experts existed to dig up and study lost civilizations in a proper manner.

This unfortunate situation began to change in 1763. In that year, Johann J. Winckelmann, a German librarian fascinated by antiquities (the name then used for ancient artifacts), began to investigate Pompeii and Herculaneum. Although he made some mistakes and drew some wrong conclusions, Winckelmann laid the initial, crucial groundwork for a new science—archaeology (a term derived from two Greek words meaning "to talk about ancient things"). His book, *History of the Art of Antiquity*, became a model for the first generation of archaeologists to follow in their efforts to understand other lost civilizations. "With unerring sensitivity," noted scholar C.W. Ceram explains, "Winckelmann groped toward original insights, and expressed them with such power of language that the cultured European world was carried away by a wave of enthusiasm for the antique ideal. This . . . was of prime importance in shaping the course of archaeology in the following century. It demonstrated means of understanding ancient cultures through their artifacts."

In the two centuries that followed, archaeologists, historians, and other scholars began to piece together the remains of lost civilizations around the world. The glory that was Greece, the grandeur that was Rome, the cradles of human civilization in Egypt's Nile valley and Mesopotamia's Tigris-Euphrates valley, the colorful royal court of ancient China's Han Dynasty, the mysterious stone cities of the Maya and Aztecs in Central America—all of these and many more were revealed in fascinating, often startling, if sometimes incomplete detail by the romantic adventure of archaeological research. This work, which continues, is vital. "Digs are in progress all over the world," says Ceram. "For we need to understand the past five thousand years in order to master the next hundred years."

Each volume in the *Lost Civilizations* series examines the history, works, everyday life, and importance of ancient cultures. The archaeological discoveries and methods used to gather this knowledge are stressed throughout. Where possible, quotes by the ancients themselves, and also by later historians, archaeologists, and other experts support and enliven the text. Primary and secondary sources are carefully documented by footnotes and each volume supplies the reader with an extensive Works Consulted list. These and other research tools afford the reader a thorough understanding of how a civilization that was long lost has once more seen the light of day and begun to reveal its secrets to its captivated modern descendants.

THE LIMITATIONS OF THE SOURCES

Before the latter part of the nineteenth century, no one knew of the existence of two rich civilizations that had flourished in Greece and its coastal islands during the Bronze Age. That era, in which people used tools and weapons made of bronze (an alloy of copper and tin), had lasted from about 3000 to 1100 B.C. It had predated the more familiar civilization of classical Greece, which produced immortals such as Pericles, Sophocles, Aristotle, Plato, and Alexander the Great, by many centuries.

One of these early Greek civilizations began to emerge in 1874. That was the year that German businessman and amateur archaeologist Heinrich Schliemann started excavations at Mycenae, a site occupying a rocky hilltop in the northeastern Peloponnesus (the large peninsula that makes up the southern third of the Greek mainland). Schliemann found an ancient palace-citadel made of massive stone blocks. Other such citadels soon came to light in southern Greece; and scholars came to call their builders the Mycenaeans, after Mycenae. It later became clear to scholars that the Mycenaeans spoke an early form of Greek.

The other Bronze Age civilization in Greece was centered on Crete, the large island lying about a hundred miles southeast of the Peloponnesus. In 1900 excavations at Knossos (or Knossus), near the island's northern coast, began to reveal an immense palace dating from the Mycenaean era. At first, the head of the dig, English scholar and excavator Sir Arthur Evans, thought he had found more Mycenaean remains. But it soon became clear that Crete had been the stronghold of a different people. Evans called them the Minoans, after Minos, a Cretan king mentioned prominently in ancient Greek myths. Since Evans's day, several more Minoan palaces and other structures and artifacts have been discovered. These reveal a prosperous, artistically vibrant people who traded with neighboring states as far away as Egypt and for several centuries exerted potent cultural, and perhaps for a while political, influence over the Mycenaeans.

A People Without a History

Unfortunately, despite more than a century of continuous excavations across Crete and nearby islands, knowledge of the Minoans remains rather limited. Other than a handful of names mentioned in myths, which may be fabricated, no political leaders or other important Minoan persons are known. Similarly, scholars know practically nothing about Minoan history. This is not simply because the Minoans lived so long ago. After all, we know the names, as well as many of the details of the conquests and other major deeds, of a number of Egyptian and Mesopotamian leaders who lived long before the Knossos palace was built.

The main problem for modern archaeologists and scholars who study the Minoans is that, unlike the Egyptians and the Mesopotamians, the Minoans left behind no written literature. The latter did possess a form of writing. But it was rudimentary and used only for recording long and tedious lists of agricultural products, livestock, and other material goods collected and stored in the palace-centers. The result, as researcher Maitland A. Edey points out, is that

> the Minoans are the only literate, highly civilized people in the world who appear to have had no sense of history whatsoever. Names and dates meant so little to them that they left no single written record that includes either. . . . Vivid though the Minoans may be in those aspects of themselves that they do reveal . . . in the end they emerge as two-dimensional: elegant, graceful, humorous, but enigmatic [mysterious]. If there were a single name . . . one flesh-and-blood personality warmed by lusts and conquests, cooled by failures, who could be squeezed out of a couple of thousand years of Minoan history, that disembodied, impersonal feeling might go away. But there is

Much of what is known about the Minoans' world comes from their surviving frescoes. This one, the Partridge Fresco, shows birds common to ancient Crete.

none. The Minoans, from the moment they appear on the world stage, to the moment they depart from it, remain anonymous.[1]

This means that scholars must rely mainly on archaeological evidence—ruined buildings, pottery, sculptures, paintings, and other artifacts—to piece together a picture of Minoan society. Fortunately, much such evidence has been found, and more comes to light each year. This evidence includes —in addition to the palaces—farmhouses, town houses, and religious shrines; cups, bowls, and storage jars; jewelry, bathtubs, toilets, grooming items, and other personal artifacts; and figurines and paintings showing Minoan people, their animals, their ships, and the landscapes in which they dwelled.

Are Traditional Views of the Minoans Realistic?

On the surface, these artifacts seem to reveal important aspects of the Minoan character. This is especially true of the paintings, which show people who were seemingly happy and carefree, connected to and in love with nature, and interested primarily in peaceful, constructive pursuits. This is certainly the traditional image of the Minoans portrayed by Evans and other scholars during much of the twentieth century. Rodney Castleden, a noted scholar of the Minoans, sums up that image (without necessarily accepting its validity) this way:

The Minoans were talented, subtle, luxury-loving, worldly, sophisticated. They were sensitive, elegant, and graceful; they loved refined and sumptuous décor, beautiful art ob-

jects, and jewelry. They loved peace and the rule of law, detesting tyranny and warfare. They had no personal ambition. . . . There were no boastful lists of great achievements or conquests. . . . Above all, the Minoans have been seen as nature-lovers. They responded to all the various aspects of the natural world: plants, flowers, and animals, birds, fish, and landscape, sea, shells, rocks, and seaweed. The princes and great ladies of the Minoan courts wandered . . . amid flowers, birds, and butterflies in their royal gardens. The Minoans were great admirers of the human body. . . . They liked to see long, slender, graceful but muscular limbs . . . on both men and women. . . . Minoan women were elegant, graceful, poised, well-mannered, and sexually alluring.[2]

But how accurate is this remarkably pleasant and docile image of the Minoans? Is it realistic that all, or even most, Minoans were like those shown in their paintings, sculpture, and other art? In the last few decades of the twentieth century an increasing number of scholars came to feel that this portrayal of the Minoans should not be taken too literally. Once more, the problem is the limitations of the surviving sources. The fact is that artistic renderings of any people or society are bound to be selective, representational, and subjective rather than completely realistic.

For example, in 1983 scholar Lucia Nixon suggested that the frequent nature motifs in Minoan art can be misleading. She pointed to the widespread use of flowers, ivy, and people lounging in meadows on china

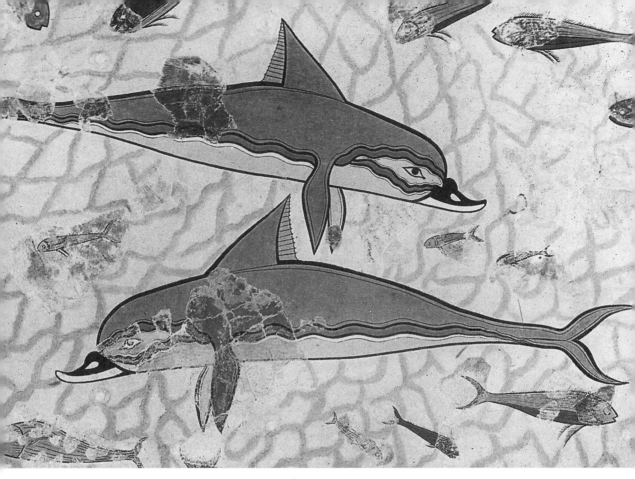

The Dolphin Fresco, found at Knossos (in northern Crete), dates from about 1600 B.C. The Minoans frequently featured aquatic themes in their art.

and wallpaper, as well as in paintings, in late nineteenth-century English art. Imagine archaeologists three thousand years from now digging up London. If they found only these flowery artistic renderings, they might well conclude that the nineteenth-century English were nature lovers incapable of the widespread environmental destruction actually wrought by the Industrial Revolution in England during those years.

Likewise, consider the same future archaeologists excavating American towns of the 1930s era. Americans in those days were hugely preoccupied with going to the movies (creating attendance records that have yet to be broken) and playing games like bingo and Monopoly (with giant tournaments of each held each year across the country). If this was the only cultural evidence the future diggers found, they might be inclined to draw a picture of Americans of that decade as pleasure seekers in a carefree age. The reality, of course, is that a worldwide depression was in full swing, and many people pursued films and games as a way of getting their minds off their poverty and other miseries.

Europe's First Advanced Culture

Therefore, archaeologists and other scholars must be very careful in interpreting the artistic evidence from Knossos and other

Minoan sites. It is probable, and indeed very likely, that the Minoans suffered from many of the same social and personal ills and problems that other ancient and modern peoples have; and that they simply chose to represent mainly the least troubling aspects of their world in their art. In fact, recent evidence, supplemented by reinterpretations of older evidence, suggests that they did use military force to further their political and other aims, which may have been more ambitious and self-serving than their tranquil and charming art would suggest.

Still, there seems little doubt that the Minoans were an energetic and passionate people who lived lives no less full than those of today's most active peoples and individuals. More importantly, Minoan society was the first advanced culture in Europe. At a time when most other sections of the continent languished in Stone Age conditions, the residents of Knossos and other Cretan sites had palaces featuring hundreds of rooms, magnificent wall paintings, a system of writing (however limited in its use), and plumbing systems on a par with many of the best in use in nineteenth-century England and America. At the dawn of the twenty-first century, historians and other scholars are hopeful that ongoing archaeological digs will reveal new sources of information about this mysterious and fascinating people whose civilization was a major basis for the myths of the later classical Greeks. In Castleden's words:

> There are great gaps in our knowledge of the Minoans, and we have to be ready to modify our view of them in the light of new archaeological discoveries. Minoan archaeology is still exceedingly young and we can be sure that many new and unexpected things remain to be learned about this remarkable civilization. Its most disappointing feature is the absence of literature. . . . Let us hope that somewhere in Crete, perhaps buried among the rubbled foundations of some yet undiscovered and unplundered temple, there is a cache of Minoan poetry [or] history.[3]

CHAPTER ONE

ARTHUR EVANS AND THE DISCOVERY OF MINOAN CIVILIZATION

Before modern historians and other scholars knew of the existence of the enigmatic Minoans, most of what was known about Bronze Age Crete was the stuff of legend. Myths told of a populous, prosperous society ruled by kings who intimidated the mainland Greeks until the Athenian hero Theseus traveled to Crete and defeated the islanders. It is important to remember that the knowledge of prehistoric Crete possessed by the classical Greeks (who built the magnificent Parthenon temple and conquered the Persian Empire) was similarly limited to these same myths. They were part of a large collection of myths and legends that told of the deeds and adventures of gods, kings, and heroes who lived long before the classical Greeks in what they called the Age of Heroes.

Modern scholars now know that the so-called Age of Heroes was really the Greek Bronze Age. They also know that two culturally advanced peoples—the Mycenaeans and the Minoans—dominated that age and that when their civilization declined, Greece entered a dark age lasting several centuries. During those years, people across the Greek world fell into a state of illiteracy and extreme poverty and largely forgot their heritage. Eventually, all that was remembered of the Bronze Age Greeks were stories handed down by word of mouth over many generations; these tales naturally became more exaggerated and embellished with each telling.

In this way, a few intriguing tales of kings, heroes, and monsters in ancient Crete made their way into the collected literature of Western (European-based) culture. And these stories were part of what inspired some nineteenth-century excavators, including the great Arthur Evans, to dig in Crete. One of Evans's contemporaries, Germany's Heinrich Schliemann, had been similarly inspired by tales of the famous Trojan War and had come to believe that the legendary city of Troy had been a real place. In 1870 Schliemann shocked the scholarly world when he uncovered the ruins of Troy in northwestern Turkey (called Asia Minor in ancient times). Soon afterward he brought to light the mighty citadel at Mycenae (on the Greek mainland), another city mentioned prominently in the folklore of the Age of Heroes. Scholars and archaeologists, who before Schliemann's achievements had assumed the Greek myths had no basis in fact, now began scrambling to mount new expeditions to find legendary cities and palaces.

This nineteenth-century drawing shows archaeologist Heinrich Schliemann sketching the ruins at Troy. Schliemann showed that myths can be based on fact.

It was this wave of enthusiasm that Evans rode to his historic discovery of the palace-center at Knossos in 1900. The structures and artifacts he found, along with those excavated later by others in Crete and nearby islands, showed that a splendid civilization once existed in the area. Though exaggerated and distorted, the old legends had indeed been based in fact. Scholars determined that the Minoans had exerted a strong influence on the mainland Mycenaeans and that the latter had eventually invaded Crete, facts that roughly correlated with events in the myths. In the space of only one generation, Evans and other researchers opened a new chapter in Greek and Western history, one that is still being written. It is perhaps appropriate to call it Chapter 1 since it describes Europe's first advanced cultures.

Land of the Minotaur

The preface, so to speak, to Europe's Chapter 1 consisted of the old myths about Crete, which turned out to have at least some basis in fact. The first writer to mention the legendary Cretans was the renowned storyteller Homer, who may have lived during the eighth century B.C. His epic poems, the *Iliad* and the *Odyssey*, were the first, and still rank among the greatest, examples of Western literature. The *Iliad*, which strongly inspired Schliemann, describes a key episode in the Trojan War; the *Odyssey* tells of the adventures of Odysseus, one of the Greek kings who besieged Troy; and both epics provide a rich fabric of information about the Greek lands and leaders of that dimly remembered age.

One of these lands, according to Homer, was Crete, and one of its leaders was the legendary King Minos. In the nineteenth book of the *Odyssey*, Odysseus says:

> Out in the dark blue sea there lies a land called Crete, a rich and lovely land, washed by the waves on every side, densely peopled and boasting ninety cities. Each of the several races of the isle has its own language. First, there are the Achaeans; then the genuine Cretans, proud of their native stock. . . . One of the ninety towns is the great city called Knossos, and there, for nine years, King Minos ruled and enjoyed the friendship of almighty Zeus [leader of the gods worshipped by the classical Greeks].[4]

What did Evans and the scholars who succeeded him make of this passage? First, they could not say for sure if a king named Minos ever existed since no direct evidence had been found for him. Some thought that the name *Minos* might have been a royal title or perhaps a family name used by a number of Cretan rulers.

A SCHOLAR HAUNTED BY CRETE

In her book about the great English archaeologist Arthur Evans and his work (written in 1943, two years after his death), his sister Joan Evans wrote about how, throughout the 1890s, he displayed an increasing interest in Crete and the possibility that new knowledge of prehistoric Greece might be revealed by excavating there.

> A new vision was beginning to haunt him: Crete. It is hard to say what chance had first drawn his attention to the unknown island. It seems as if a thousand tiny facts and things had drifted like dust and settled to weigh down the scales of his decision. His father's acquaintance, Henry [Heinrich] Schliemann, had revealed a bright new world by his excavations at Troy, Mycenae [and other Bronze Age sites]. There seemed, especially at Mycenae, to be things of many dates, drawn from various sources; and those sources were for the most part unknown. Schliemann had planned to excavate "broad Knossos" [in northern Crete], but had never done so. And now the same avowed intention was drawing on the mind of Arthur Evans. On February 3, 1892, he was in Rome, and made friends with . . . an Italian archaeologist who had already explored many of the classical sites in Crete. What he told him of the earlier remains on the island, unexplored and unexplained, fired his imagination and confirmed his interest, though as yet his purpose was hardly formed.

In any case, archaeology has shown that much of the rest of the Homeric passage is factually sound. Knossos *was* the most prominent of many Cretan towns, and the island was indeed densely populated and economically prosperous. The reference to different races and languages also rings true. Scholars now know that Homer's Achaeans, whom he said sacked Troy, were Mycenaean Greeks, who also took over Crete and thereafter dominated the natives.

A more detailed and important legend of early Crete involved the Athenian hero Theseus. In the story, every nine years the rulers of Knossos demanded and received from Athens a ransom consisting of fourteen young men and women. The captives were taken to the Labyrinth, a huge building featuring a maze of rooms and corridors. And there they became the unfortunate victims of the Minotaur, a fearsome creature described as half man and half bull. According to the first-century A.D. Greek writer Plutarch in his biography of Theseus, "When these young men and women reached Crete, they were thrown into the Labyrinth and there killed by the Minotaur, or else wandered about and finally perished because they could find no way out."[5] Eventually, as recalled in the myth, Theseus went to Crete, fought the Cretans, entered the Labyrinth, and slew the Minotaur, thereby putting an end to the threat posed to Athens by the Cretan regime.

Knossos Emerges from the Earth

This famous story about the Labyrinth, the bull-monster that inhabited it, and Theseus's triumph over the creature remained a mere fable until Arthur Evans began excavating the palace at Knossos. Hailing from a wealthy English family, Evans served as director of a museum in Oxford before traveling extensively in Greece and other parts of the eastern Mediterranean region. At first, he was mainly interested in collecting small ancient Greek artifacts, especially gemlike seals (small carvings used to make impressions in wax) that bore carved seascapes and hunting scenes. These seemed unusually numerous in the Aegean Islands. In addition, the old myths telling of many prosperous cities in ancient Crete led Evans to believe he might find plentiful artifacts on that island.

During his stay in Crete, Evans visited the low, broad mound of Kephala (near the northern coast), which had long been seen as the traditional site of ancient Knossos. It was clear (from scattered, exposed walls and other artifacts) that some kind of extensive ruins lay just beneath the surface there; and he found himself gripped with the desire to excavate the mound. It took six years of complicated negotiations with the local authorities before he was allowed to break ground on the site, an event that occurred on March 23, 1900.

In large part because the dirt and other debris covering the ruins was so shallow, the work proceeded quickly. Evans started out with a handful of helpers. But as the huge size of the ruins became clear, he quickly expanded his staff to more than a hundred. Steadily, the remains of an ancient palace complex covering more than three acres met the light of day for the first time in thousands of years. Noted scholar Richard Ellis provides this excellent general description of Evans's discovery:

> The palace itself covers an area of some 22,000 square meters (26,312 square yards) and is constructed of

A watercolor completed in 1935 captures Sir Arthur Evans's vision of what the palace-center at Knossos, which he excavated, looked like in its heyday.

stone, wood, and clay. (Eventually, the palace would be shown to include more than a thousand rooms.) The plan, such as it was, appears to consist of multi-storied royal apartments, storerooms, religious shrines, great halls, capacious [broad and roomy] staircases, rooms, and courtyards randomly added to the central court, which is about 50 yards long and half as wide. . . . The rooms were connected by light wells—small courtyards that allowed light to enter roofed-over areas. This meant that no section was ever in darkness, no matter how intricate the plan. At the greatest height, the palace was five stories tall. . . . The upper floors were supported by wooden columns . . . [and] the walls were made of rubble masonry or mud brick, framed with horizontal timbers, and plastered.[6]

Comparing the Legends to Reality

Evans and other scholars who gazed on these emerging remains of the great palace were struck by how closely the reality of this portion of prehistoric Crete matched many aspects of the legends. Bulls, including the monstrous Minotaur, had played a major role in the Cretan myths. And Evans found paintings, sculptures, and other representations of bulls everywhere in the Knossos ruins. Large upraised masonry horns decorated the tops of walls and buildings, while one of the major entrances to the palace complex bore a striking relief sculpture of a bull. "It is life-sized, or somewhat over, and modeled in high relief," Evans later wrote.

> It is the most magnificent monument of Mycenaean plastic art that has come down to our time . . . full of life and spirit. [When he wrote this, near the start of his excavations, Evans

---

EVANS DESCRIBES
THE SITE OF KNOSSOS

During his excavations at Knossos, Arthur Evans sent regular reports of his progress to be published in the prestigious *Annual of the British School at Athens*. In this installment, which appeared in the 1899–1900 issue, he describes the attributes of the site where he was beginning to unearth a huge Bronze Age palace.

> The site of ancient Knossos . . . about four miles inland from [the coast] is shut in by hills in three directions. Somewhat south, however . . . the ground gradually rises into a rounded hill generally known as Kephala. . . . This hill lies at the confluence of a tributary stream . . . and descends somewhat steeply towards these channels on the south and east. To the west of the hill . . . runs a road, the antiquity of which is shown by the rock tombs that extend along its further course. This road must in all ages of Cretan history have formed the natural lines of access [to sites farther inland]. . . . Although overlooked by loftier heights beyond the streams and the road, the partial isolation of the hill of Kephala, and the fact that it immediately commanded this natural line of communication, must have made it in early times something of key position.

---

still thought the builders were Mycenaeans.] It combines in a high degree naturalism with grandeur, and it is no exaggeration to say that no figure of a bull at once so powerful and so true was produced by later classical [Greek] art. . . . What a part these creatures [bulls] play here! . . . Was not one or other of these creatures [the inspiration for the] tradition of the Bull of Minos [in the myths]?[7]

Another correlation between the palace and the legends was the structure's size, complexity, and obvious function as a major seat of power. Its hundreds of seemingly randomly placed rooms and corridors on multiple levels recalled the famous Labyrinth in the Theseus myth. Moreover, the richly decorated apartments confirmed that a king or other powerful leader—if not Minos himself, someone like him—dwelled in the structure.

However, it soon became clear to Evans that the so-called palace he was uncovering was not simply a royal residence. It was also the administrative center of the local economy; and subsequent evidence has shown that it was probably a central religious shrine as well. For this reason, scholars came to call the Knossos structure a palace-center (later also applied to similar structures unearthed elsewhere in Crete) to distinguish it from a mere residential palace.

For Evans and other scholars the sheer size and complexity of the emerging palace-center, as well as its geographic placement, seemed to confirm claims in the myths about Knossos being the center of a populous, strong, and prosperous kingdom. It would certainly have to be all of these things in order to impose its will on the mainlanders, as claimed in the Theseus story. Archaeologists refer to such large-scale architecture as "monumental" and point out that a great deal can be deduced about any nation or people that employs it. "Monumentality is significant," says University of California, Los Angeles, archaeologist Louise A. Hitchcock,

in that it implies planning, full-time craftsmen, and the organization of materials and labor. Each of these factors implies a high level of social complexity that requires an agricultural surplus, as well as the emergence of social ranking and hierarchy [ladders of authority]. Symbolically, monumental structures communicate permanence, power, and status. . . .

The Minoans stored large quantities of food and other commodities in their palace-centers. This is one of the storage areas uncovered at Knossos by Arthur Evans.

Also notable . . . is the placement of the palaces within the landscape. Their frequent orientation to sacred mountains housing peak and/or cave sanctuaries, was connected with the religious beliefs of the populace, and their coastal locations communicated prestige to visiting traders.[8]

Evidence of Sophisticated Urban Life

This supposition that the Minoans, as Evans eventually came to call them, had created a splendid, powerful civilization long before the rise of classical Greece was increasingly confirmed as his diggers revealed more and more of the Knossos palace-center. The structure had many large storage areas for grain, olives and olive oil, grapes and wine, and other foodstuffs as well as weapons and other goods. Scholars agreed that the immense amount of goods stored could only have been produced by hundreds or thousands of workers coordinated by whoever ran the palace-center. Evans wondered if this powerful person had held audiences in a room unearthed in the first year of excavation. Evans assumed it was a throne room because he found a thronelike stone seat still intact against a wall that was originally covered with colorful paintings. His sister, Joan Evans, later recorded his description of the chamber:

On the other side of the north wall was a short bench, like that of the outer chamber, and then separated from it by a small interval a separate seat of honor or throne. It had a high back . . . which was partly imbedded

The ruins of the palace-center at Kato Zakro, in eastern Crete, look less imposing than those at Knossos, partly because some of the latter have been reconstructed.

in the stucco of the wall. It was raised on a square base and had a curious molding below the crockets [leaflike ornaments]. (Almost Gothic!)[9]

Evans and his assistants were also thrilled to find the remnants of many magnificent frescoes (paintings done on wet plaster). These renderings, a number of which still retained bright colors, depict Minoans, male and female, engaged in various activities. Some of these activities are apparently religious in nature, others perhaps secular (nonreligious). Many show large crowds of people engaged in communal gatherings, including watching sporting events.

Other evidence for urban life and skilled craftsmen at Knossos consisted of the remains of sophisticated plumbing facilities that provided running water and efficient waste removal. Pipes made of ceramics (like the vases and storage jars) carried water from room to room. These pipes tapered at the ends so that they could slide into the ends of others. Also, separate built-in stone drains ran beneath floors and courtyards. "There were even toilets," Maitland Edey writes,

> evidence of which is preserved in traces of seats over large drains that lead outside the palace. Wastes were flushed away by pouring water down an elaborate system of drains that included clay pipes carefully fitted together in sections and stone troughs to carry off rain water. The bathtubs, however, did not connect with the pipes. They were large comfortable affairs of glazed clay, often brightly decorated with pictures of fish and dolphins. Plugless, they apparently were bailed or sponged out by a ser-

vant when the bather was through washing, [and] the dirty water [was] thrown down the nearest drain.[10]

Other Minoan Palaces and Towns Revealed

These marvels unearthed by Evans proved to be only the tip of the iceberg, so to speak, of Minoan archaeological discoveries. Within months of his discovery of the great palace-center at Knossos, two similar, though smaller, versions were found by other archaeologists. One emerged at Phaistos, on Crete's southern coast; the other, which may have been a summer residence for the rulers at Phaistos, is located at Hagia Triada, only a few miles west of Phaistos. (Some scholars think the Hagia Triada structure is too small to qualify as a palace-center, so they refer to it as a *mansion*.) In 1915 a fourth palace-center was discovered at Mallia, on the northern coast east of Knossos. And in 1961 archaeologist Nicolas Platon began excavating the palace-center of Kato Zakro, which has yielded an unusual number of well-preserved tools and personal artifacts. "Kato Zakro lies at the extreme eastern tip of Crete," Edey writes,

> walled off from the rest of the island by high mountains. . . . [The palace-center] fell in a single, violent instant that left [it] a smoking ruin. Its inhabitants fled and never went back. As a result, excavators of the site have found things there in an abundance that no other palace has provided: tools . . . household objects, kitchen equipment, bits of food—all scattered wildly and untouched since the day of destruction.[11]

In addition to these major palace-centers (and some others discovered more recently), archaeologists who poured over Crete during the twentieth century found the remains of a number of Minoan houses and villages. They also discovered small settlements displaying Minoan-like architecture and artifacts on nearby islands. In 1967 Greek archaeologist Spyridon Marinatos found a large town of this type on the small island of Santorini (called Thera in ancient times), lying about seventy miles directly north of Crete. Some of these island settlements may have been Minoan colonies founded by the rulers at Knossos and the other palace-centers; but evidence suggests that many were independent island cultures that adopted Minoan dress, social customs, and artistic styles. Whatever their status, Evans and other scholars viewed them as evidence for a powerful Crete-based Bronze Age maritime empire very much like that described in the myths. Its influence extended to the Greek mainland as well, where the Mycenaeans adopted Minoan customs and styles at least by the sixteenth century B.C.

Dating Aegean and Minoan Civilization

Thus, as the remnants of a Bronze Age civilization in Greece and the Aegean Islands emerged, scholars discerned three main cultural spheres. The culture in each was very similar to those in the others, yet still retained some local differences. These spheres were: Crete, the center of Minoan culture; the other southern Aegean Islands, called the Cyclades, which were controlled or at least highly "Minoanized" by the Cretans; and the southeastern coastal portions of the mainland, where the Mycenaeans held sway.

For the sake of convenience, archaeologists developed three separate dating systems for these cultural spheres in the Bronze Age. The Cretan chronology is called, appropriately, Minoan; the island one is called Cycladic; and the mainland one is dubbed Helladic (but is also sometimes called Mycenaean). Each of these chronologies breaks down further into Early, Middle, and Late periods.

For Evans and other archaeologists who pioneered the discovery of the Minoan sites in Crete, the Minoan chronology was the more important of the three dating systems. As worked out by Evans (and later refined by other experts), the Early Minoan (EM) Period began in about 3000 B.C. and marked the beginning of the Bronze Age in Crete (and in the rest of the Aegean region). Evans and other scholars found evidence that the Minoans already inhabited Crete by this time. In fact, the Minoans seem to have been there as early as 6000 B.C., subsisting by hunting, gathering, and rudimentary agriculture. No one knows where they came from. But the scholarly consensus is that they originally migrated in small boats from the coast of Asia Minor.

The Early Minoan Period ended and the Middle Minoan (MM) Period began in about 2200 B.C. or somewhat later. At this time in Crete there was a rapid rise in population, the appearance of large towns, expanded trade and manufacturing of trade goods, and the erection of the first versions of the palace-centers. These centers underwent periodic cycles of damage by earthquakes, followed by rebuilding, in the next few centuries.

The end of the MM Period and start of the Late Minoan (LM) Period took place in

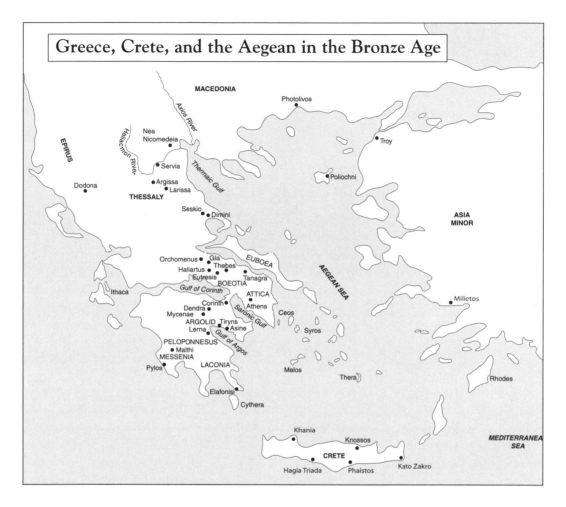

Greece, Crete, and the Aegean in the Bronze Age

about 1550 B.C. In their final era, the Minoans were in decline, and for most of the LM Period Knossos and much of the rest of Crete were dominated by mainland Mycenaeans. The end of the LM Period, and of Minoan civilization itself, occurred between 1200 and 1100 B.C., when all of the Aegean Bronze Age cultures collapsed and disappeared forever, for reasons that are still uncertain and somewhat mysterious.[12]

The unanswered questions about the Minoans and their demise underscore that much remains unknown about them. What is known has been pieced together by hundreds of scholars and excavators over the course of more than a century. Yet all involved were (or are now) aware of the tremendous debt owed to Arthur Evans. He excavated diligently in Crete for thirty-five years, and his mammoth *The Palace of Minos at Knossos*, published between 1921 and 1936, remains the bible of Minoan studies. "The scope of the undertaking is staggering," says archaeologist Alexandre Farnoux. "It is the work of a pioneer who laid the groundwork of all future Minoan archaeology."[13]

CHAPTER TWO

FARMING, FINANCES, AND TRADE IN MINOAN CRETE

The remains of Minoan civilization excavated to date reveal a sophisticated, thriving society with royal courts, large-scale architecture, cities and towns, networks of roads, seaports and fleets of ships, advanced crafts and trades, and magnificent works of art. Such a complex, prosperous society cannot exist without certain basic requirements. It must have a population large enough to supply the workers and defenders needed to perpetuate the community, for example. A prosperous society must also constantly look for and exploit a wide range of natural resources and accumulate considerable amounts of supplies and wealth to sustain itself in lean years.

What resources, both natural and human, did the Minoans exploit? And what were the main elements of their economy? Here, it is important not to interpret the word *economy* in the modern sense—that is, as an organized national or local scheme having a formal set of financial goals and measures or a reasoned theory about how a state or community might become financially prosperous. Ancient societies did not have this level of economic theory and planning. When modern scholars discuss the economy of an ancient people they do so informally, as a kind of shorthand to denote the general realm of finances and making a living.

One way the Minoans made their living was through trade. The fifth-century B.C. Athenian historian Thucydides wrote that the famous mythical King Minos opened new settlements and trade routes in the Aegean region. However, to control and exploit the Aegean seaways, Minos first needed to deal with gangs of pirates who menaced the region. "Minos, according to tradition, was the first person to organize a navy," Thucydides says.

> He controlled the greater part of what is now the Hellenic Sea [today called the Aegean Sea]. He ruled over the Cyclades, in most of which he founded the first colonies, putting his sons in as governors. . . . And it is reasonable to suppose that he did his best to put down piracy in order to secure his own revenues [from overseas trade]. For in these early times, as communication by sea became easier, so piracy became a common profession both among the Greeks and among the barbarians [non-Greeks] who lived on the coasts and in the islands [of the Aegean].[14]

Thucydides went on to say that Minos used his navy to drive out the worst pirates. This naturally had the effect of making the settlements on nearby islands and coastlines safer and better able to carry on regular trade with Knossos and other Minoan towns.

It is important to emphasize that Thucydides lived more than six centuries after the collapse and disappearance of the Minoans and other Bronze Age residents of Greece. Like other classical Greeks, he did not know who these peoples really were, exactly when they lived, or the details of their societies and economies. To him, Minos, Theseus, and other notables from the old myths were simply earlier Greeks who had established Greece's major cities, trades, and social customs. Thucydides did not realize that Crete

had been dominated by various and separate palace-centers, each of which had developed a local economy of its own. Only in modern times did it become clear that the ruler (or rulers) of each palace-center tightly controlled both local agriculture and overseas trade to keep society and the government solvent and running efficiently.

Still, Thucydides did know that the inhabitants of Crete in the Age of Heroes were prosperous traders who extended their economic and other influence throughout the Aegean sphere and beyond. He probably acquired this knowledge from stories and traditions that had been handed down through the ages orally, including Homer's epics and other sources now lost. Though riddled with exaggerations and fabrications, these accounts

Trade goods were stored in these large jars, found at Akrotiri, on the island of Thera, which was apparently a Minoan colony or ally in the Bronze Age.

MAKING THE SEAWAYS SAFE FOR TRADE

In his famous book about the ruinous Peloponnesian War, the fifth-century B.C. Athenian historian Thucydides discusses conditions in Greece during the era that Greeks of his day called the Age of Heroes. In this passage (from Rex Warner's translation), he tells how the legendary King Minos improved safety and brought about economic expansion by ridding the seaways of the serious pirate menace.

In these early times, as communication by sea became easier, so piracy became a common profession both among the Greeks and among the barbarians [non-Greeks] who lived on the coast and in the islands. The leading pirates were powerful men, acting both out of self-interest and in order to support the weak among their own people. They would descend upon cities which were unprotected by walls . . . and by plundering such places they would gain most of their livelihood. . . . Because of the wide prevalence of piracy, the ancient cities, both in the islands and on the mainland, were built at some distance from the sea. . . . For the pirates would rob not only each other, but everyone else, seafaring or not, who lived along the coasts. . . . But after Minos had organized a navy, sea communications improved. He sent colonies to most of the islands and drove out the notorious pirates, with the result that those who lived on the sea-coasts were now in a position to acquire wealth and live a more settled life.

Ships extremely similar to these ancient Egyptian vessels are depicted in several ancient Minoan frescoes.

also contain (or contained) factual elements, including references to colonies, fleets, trade, and pirates in the dim past.

The Cretan Collectives

Before the discovery of the Minoan palace-centers during the twentieth century, these scattered ancient mythical accounts and a few brief passages in the works of Thucydides and other classical Greek writers contained all that scholars knew about how people in the Bronze Age Aegean made their livings. A number of scholars assumed that people in that bygone era sustained themselves the same way the classical Greeks did. Namely, the Greeks of Thucydides' day were mostly independent farmers and herders who sold or traded their products at market. This mode of exchange, supplemented by overland or overseas trade with other cities and foreign lands, constituted an early kind of capitalism, or free-market economy.

Once Arthur Evans and his colleagues began unearthing and studying the Cretan palace-centers, however, it quickly became clear that the Minoans did not have a free-market system. Instead, their economy was collective, or redistributive, in nature. A socioeconomic collective is a society or group in which all members labor or produce goods for the greater community rather than to further their own aims. A central authority directs the labor, collects the goods, and then redistributes some of them back to the people, usually only as needed. The small agricultural communes operating in Israel and a few other modern nations are familiar examples.

In Bronze Age Crete, each palace-center appears to have been the central authority of a local collective; the king, or perhaps the high priest or priestess of the state religion, aided by his or her leading nobles, decided what and how much the farmers and crafts-people should produce. In the words of noted scholar Thomas R. Martin of the College of the Holy Cross:

> The central authority told producers how much they had to contribute to the central collection facility and also decided what each member of the society would receive for subsistence and reward. In other words, the palaces did not support a market economy. . . . The Cretan redistributive arrangement required both ingenuity and complicated administration. To handle receipt and disbursement [handing out] of olive oil and wine, for example, the palaces had vast storage areas filled with hundreds of gigantic jars next to storerooms crammed with bowls, cups, and dippers. Scribes meticulously recorded what came in and what went out by writing on clay tablets kept in the palace. This process of economic redistribution applied to craft specialists as well as food producers, and the palace's administrative officials set specifications for craft-producers' contributions, which amounted to work quotas.[15]

Some scholars point out that it is possible that rural Minoans sometimes traded or bartered goods with one another in deals separate from the palace-based system. However, all the available evidence suggests that in each region of Crete the collective was the mainstay of the economy and overshadowed any supplementary financial dealings on the fringes of society.

Minoan Villages and Farmhouses

For such an agricultural collective to function, it is necessary for the bulk of the local population to be farmers, along with a smaller number of people involved in crafts and trades. In fact, this conforms to established patterns for other ancient societies. The vast majority of the inhabitants of ancient Mesopotamia, Egypt, classical Greece, and Roman Italy were farmers and herders; and there is every reason to believe that the Minoans (and their neighbors, the Mycenaeans) were no different.

As for how many Minoans lived and worked in the countryside, in contrast to in the towns, no one can say for sure. Population estimates made by scholars in 2001 for the town of Knossos at its height range from fourteen thousand to eighteen thousand. Assuming these figures are correct, it is likely that at least twice that number of people dwelled in the villages and farmsteads in the surrounding countryside. Factoring in the rural farming regions surrounding the other palace-centers, it would probably be safe to say that in its heyday Minoan Crete supported an agricultural base of more than one hundred thousand people, and perhaps more than two hundred thousand.

Some of these country folk lived in small villages. The village of Myrtos (on Crete's southern coast west of Kato Zakro), excavated between 1967 and 1968, appears to have been fairly typical. Its human population was about thirty. The residents walked to their nearby fields each morning, where they grew cereal grains and pastured sheep, goats, and cattle. Most of the grain, wool,

and hides thus produced, along with clay and stone figurines made in the village, were likely collected by agents from the palace-center. (It was either the one at Phaistos or Kato Zakro; Myrtos lies almost halfway between the two, and it is unknown to which center the village owed its allegiance.)

Other rural Minoans had separate farmhouses right beside or in the midst of their fields and pasturelands. A Minoan farmhouse, made of fieldstones, has been excavated about an hour's walk south of the Phaistos palace-center. It had a central living room covering about sixty square feet (about the size of a small bedroom in a modern American home). The floor was made of hard-beaten earth, and a wooden pillar supported the ceiling. Six smaller rooms—probably a mix of bedrooms and storerooms—were arranged on either side of the central room. No evidence of a kitchen has been found, so the occupants must have cooked their food on a hearth in the open air. The remains of other Minoan rural houses have been found, some built around small central courtyards and featuring crude kitchens (which had stone hearths for cooking); a few even had partial second stories. These houses were fairly roomy and comfortable, and very well built and durable, which suggests that most Minoan peasants did not live in abject poverty, as was the case in many other ancient societies.

Common Crops

The residents of these rural houses raised a number of different crops. The principal ones were grains, of which there is evidence for two or more varieties of wheat, along with spelt and barley. The first step in growing such crops was to clear trees and under-

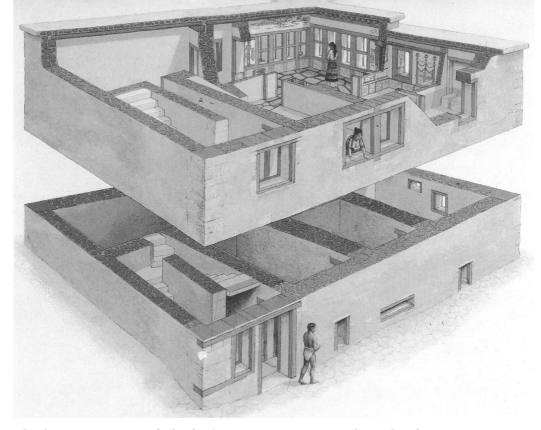

This drawing reconstructs the levels of a two-story Minoan town house, based on surviving remains unearthed at Akrotiri.

growth from a patch of land. This was accomplished using axes, each of which consisted of a wooden handle attached by leather thongs to a bronze blade (via holes in the back of the blade). A similar but smaller blade on a longer handle was used for hoeing and weeding.

Once the land was cleared, a farmer turned over the earth using a wooden plow. Such plows are depicted on tablets found at Knossos and other palace-centers and appear to have consisted of three separate components joined by leather thongs. Oxen or donkeys pulled the plows. Some tablets from Knossos mention ox drivers and even their oxen by name; among the latter are Sandy, Blacky, Red, Noisy, White-Foot, and Spotty.

After the plowing, the seeds were planted. And when it was time for the harvest, the farmers cut down the grain using bronze sickles. The agents from the palace collectives gathered the grain (or the farmers themselves delivered it to the palace-centers), and before distribution it was stored in granaries. These were constructed by digging a pit, lining it with rough masonry and plaster, and covering it with a dome made of stones placed so that they slightly overlaid one another (a technique called corbeling). The remains of several granaries of this type were discovered in the palace-center at Mallia.

In addition to grains, farmers in the Minoan collectives raised peas, sesame, hemp (for making rope), flax (for making yarn), figs, grapes, and olives. Figs may well have been the Minoans' favorite fruit. The Knossos tablets mention fig trees often and list

A series of ancient Egyptian painted panels shows farmers planting and harvesting grain. Scholars think the Minoans used similar farming methods.

a single estate having 1,770 fig trees! Meanwhile, as would be true later in classical Greece, grapevines and olives grew well in the warm Mediterranean climate and were important staples. The Knossos tablets make frequent mention of vines, and it appears that wine was used in religious ceremonies; it may also have been a common beverage, although evidence for this is sketchy. As for the olive and its essential products, Rodney Castleden writes that

> olive oil was used for cooking, washing, lighting, and possibly as a body

oil. . . . The olive harvest was the last and longest of the year, starting in November and going on until the beginning of March. The olives were probably beaten from the trees with sticks, just as they are today, then soaked in water, crushed in wooden mortars or presses, and the resulting pulp put into a settling tank.[16]

Livestock and Other Animals

Also essential to the Minoan economy were various animals. Cattle, sheep, goats, and pigs were all raised in the countryside. Cattle were used not only to pull plows and wagons carrying heavy loads, but also for their milk, for their skins (which were cured and stretched over wooden cores to make shields for soldiers), and as sacred animals in games and worship. Pigs were used in sacrifice as well as for eating.

Sheep were particularly numerous in ancient Crete. In fact, a good deal of evidence found in various parts of the island indicates that sheep-raising was a major industry. Sheep appear frequently in Minoan arts and crafts, for example. A clay dish discovered in the Minoan town of Palaikastro, near Crete's eastern coast, bears a representation of a shepherd and some of his sheep. And as Castleden points out, "The Knossos tablets add documentary evidence by listing very large numbers of sheep. The total mentioned for the Labyrinth's final year, around 1380 B.C., runs to about 100,000 sheep." The importance of sheep in Bronze Age Crete is emphasized by the fact that this high number was recorded at a time when Knossos was in severe decline; and that the other palace-centers, before they were abandoned, had their own large flocks. "The number of lambs are carefully noted" in the tablets, Castleden continues,

> presumably so as to keep a check on the ever-changing strength of the flocks. The tablets record target figures for flocks and for wool production. The target is one unit of wool, about three kilograms [6.6 pounds] for every four sheep . . . which agrees with the quantity of wool expected from sheep in the medieval period.[17]

Other animals that figured prominently in Minoan Crete's economy were dogs and bees. As has been the case throughout recorded history, dogs were used in hunting, which means that they helped secure valuable meat, hides, and horns. Some dogs may also have helped herd goats and other animals. Excavators at a Cretan site found a seal stone featuring a carving of a dog barking at a goat it had cornered on a rock. The Minoans clearly admired dogs and at least sometimes kept them as pets, as they were often the subjects of artists and craftspeople. For instance, a number of early Minoan pot lids bear carvings of dogs sitting or lying down.

Bees were important in ancient Crete because they produced the only sweetener in the Minoan diet—honey. No Minoan beehives have survived. But they are depicted in Minoan art, and bees were a common motif in jewelry, including a gold pendant showing bees kissing that was found at Mallia. (There is also the famous mythical episode in which King Minos's son, Glaukos, fell into a large jar of honey stored in the Knossos palace and drowned in it.)

Minoan Traders and Their Wares

The products mentioned so far—grains, figs, grapes, olives, honey, and various kinds of livestock—were used for more than distribution and consumption by the Cretan collectives. Along with a number of metals, crafts, and other goods, they were also used as valuable trade items.

Evidence suggests that the rise and expansion of the Minoan trading sphere, which was quite extensive for a Bronze Age culture, was in large degree stimulated by a response to population increases in Crete.

Bees played an important part in the economy of Minoan Crete. This gold pendant, showing bees kissing, was found at Mallia.

In the early Middle Minoan Period (or First Palace Period)—roughly 1900 B.C.—the island's population rose rapidly and many new towns were built. A similar but smaller rise in population and town building occurred between 1550 and 1500 B.C. It seems that the Minoans also established colonies in the Cyclades and beyond and started trading with them during these intervals. In addition, they began and maintained trading partnerships with existing non-Minoan Cycladic communities.

Also, Minoan traders made frequent trips far beyond the Cyclades. They reached mainland Greece and southern Italy in the west, Troy in northwestern Asia Minor, the coasts of southern Asia Minor, the large island of Cyprus (lying south of Asia Minor), and the coasts of Palestine and Egypt far to the south of Cyprus. Evidence for Minoan

contacts with Egypt takes the form of paintings of Minoan traders found in several Egyptian tombs. The Egyptians called the Minoans the "Keftiu." (It is unknown whether this was the Minoans' own name for themselves or whether they called themselves something else.) Harvard University scholar Emily Vermeule, one of the past century's leading experts on Bronze Age Greece, describes the physical characteristics of the Keftiu in the Egyptian paintings:

> The usual Keftiu costume [in these paintings] is a short embroidered kilt with a codpiece [covering for the genitals] or a deep tassled prong between the thighs, cinched at the waist by a broad, tooled belt of metal or leather. The Keftiu wear elaborate sandals with high ankle straps or even turned-up toes.[18]

What trading goods did the Minoans take to Egypt, Cyprus, the Greek mainland, and elsewhere? Minoan bronze swords and gold, silver, and bronze vases and other vessels have been found on the Greek mainland. And exquisite painted pottery containers made in Crete have turned up on Thera and other Cycladic islands as well as in Asia Minor and Cyprus. Archaeologists found Minoan stone lamps in the ruins of Troy, and Minoan metal vases have been found in Egypt and in the Lipari Islands (off the coast of Italy). There is little doubt that the Minoans exported perishable materials too, which have disintegrated over the centuries. Archaeologists sometimes call these "invisible" exports (or imports) because they leave behind few or no traces. They included olive oil, cloth, honey, and timber, among other goods. A major clue to the existence of such invisible commodities consists of huge surpluses in the storage areas of the palace-centers. The amounts of oil and other perishable materials stored at Knossos and recorded by the scribes often exceeds what would have been needed for the local population; a portion of each must have been earmarked for trade.

Imported Goods and Financial Dealings

In exchange for these goods, the Minoans imported many commodities from far and wide. One important item they needed from overseas was tin to make bronze. The exact sources of their tin, a rare and very valuable commodity in ancient times, are unknown, and indeed, they may not have known where the tin originated either. Evidence

EGYPTIAN DEPICTIONS OF MINOAN TRADERS

In this excerpt from her book *Greece in the Bronze Age*, noted Harvard University scholar Emily Vermeule describes the Egyptian tomb paintings that show Minoan traders (whom the Egyptians called the Keftiu).

It was the highest fashion in fifteenth-century B.C. Egypt to decorate the walls of one's funerary chamber with exotic processions of foreigners bringing expensive gifts or bowing in humility before the might of Egypt. The painters regularly included Asiatics, Syrians, Libyans, Africans, and occasionally . . . the men of Keftiu. . . . Among the foreigners, the Keftiu are surely meant to represent Cretans in Minoan costume, usually carrying elaborate metal vases, animal rhyta [drinking vessels shaped like horns], ingots, or rolls of cloth. . . . There are ten or more tombs at Thebes [one of Egypt's ancient capitals] which include Keftiu in their repertories. . . . The usual Keftiu costume [in these paintings] is a short embroidered kilt with a codpiece or a deep tassled prong between the thighs, cinched at the waist by a broad, tooled belt of metal or leather. The Keftiu wear elaborate sandals with high ankle straps or even turned-up toes. . . . They wear their hair long, and it is distinguished from other foreigners' by its wavy strands over the shoulders and a spring of spitcurls on the crown [of the head].

Some colorful frescoes found at Akrotiri, on Thera, depict monkeys. The Minoans imported these creatures, most likely from Egypt or some other part of North Africa.

shows that they received it from European merchants in southern Italy or somewhere else west of Greece; but the metal probably originated in northern Italy, Spain, or perhaps even Britain.

Other Minoan imports included ornamental stones from the Greek mainland; emery (for polishing stone bowls and vases) from the Cycladic island of Naxos; copper from Cyprus; lapis lazuli (a semiprecious stone) and ivory from Syria; and white alabaster building stones, amethysts, beads, pendants, finely made figurines, and ostrich eggs and plumes from Egypt. Invisible imports almost

certainly included yarns and fabrics, fruits and other foodstuffs that did not grow well in Crete, and exotic animals, such as monkeys (which were depicted in Minoan art).

It is natural to wonder about the nature of the actual financial dealings in the two-way trade described. Money, both coins and the paper variety, did not yet exist. It appears that the Minoans and their trading partners made even trades of goods, a basic form of barter. However, both parties had to agree on the relative values of the goods. Some scholars think they priced them by making their values equivalent to set amounts of gold or silver. It is possible, of course, that the Minoans employed a different financial system that was lost when their civilization disappeared. Or perhaps they engaged in long, complex sessions of haggling over prices. As Castelden points out:

> There is no need to suppose that the ways of the Minoan traders were simple, straightforward, or even efficient. The tablets reveal the Minoans as lovers of minutely recorded detail; their labyrinthine architecture reveals a love of complexity and puzzles. It may be that the Minoans enjoyed the social and diplomatic aspects of long-drawn-out negotiations over the price of a cargo with Egyptian, Cypriot, or Trojan merchants. That love of haggling is still there in the Mediterranean economy, and maybe it began with the Minoan traders.[19]

CHAPTER THREE

POLITICAL AND SOCIAL LIFE IN THE MINOAN TOWNS

When attempting to draw a picture of what political and social customs and other aspects of daily life were like for the Minoans, especially in the towns, modern historians and other scholars are at a severe disadvantage. It must be emphasized again that no literature or other descriptive writings from Minoan Crete have survived; and it is highly doubtful that they ever existed in the first place. The tablets found at Knossos and other palace-centers contain only inventory lists of goods of various kinds. True, these lists do reveal some interesting things about Minoan society—such as the kinds of workers and their professions, common crops, tools, and weapons—and the kind of economic system that was in place. But for other aspects of Minoan life, scholars must rely on whatever archaeology reveals.

The problem is that, in the absence of ancient personal statements by or about the Minoans, the amount of information archaeology has been able to reveal so far has been minimal. First, the ruins in question are enormously old—mostly between thirty-two hundred and forty-six hundred years old. A great amount of erosion (from rain, wind, floods, earthquakes, and air pollution) has taken place over the centuries, destroying a lot of valuable evidence pertaining to

human habits and daily life. Also, the palace-centers and some of the individual houses were burned and looted, sometimes several times, in ancient times, eradicating still more evidence. Most interior furnishings and personal items disappeared in this manner. Further complicating matters is the way the Minoans themselves eliminated evidence in the natural course of building and rebuilding their habitations. For example, Maitland Edey summarizes the sad state of the ruins at Knossos when excavators first began working there:

> Major sections of the palace had been built and rebuilt over many hundreds of years and were now in a hideous jumble. Parts of it had stood four or five stories high. When its floors had collapsed, pottery had gone plunging into basements, along with clay tablets and other objects. Walls had crashed, their stones raised at some later date for the building of new walls, then, still later, crashed again.[20]

This does not mean that piecing together any sort of picture of Minoan life is hopeless. On the plus side, physical remains of houses and their living rooms, bedrooms, and plumbing facilities give some idea of living standards and the level of creature comforts the Minoans enjoyed. And paintings, figurines, and other kinds of art are helpful. They tell something about religious practices (though little about beliefs), styles of dress and hair, and the social position of women (which appears to have been high for an ancient culture). The paintings also show what Minoan ships looked like, which offers a few clues about the lives of fishermen and traders. Other clues suggest that the largest Minoan towns (which might have been small cities) were for a long time individual city-states or small independent kingdoms. Each seems to have been controlled and administered by its palace-center and to have coexisted (and maybe at times competed) with neighboring Cretan states.

Despite these and a few other tantalizing snapshots of the Minoan towns, huge areas of society and life within them remain blank or nearly so to modern observers. Nothing

This 1941 drawing by an archaeologist reconstructs the so-called throne room at Knossos. Many experts now suspect that it was used by a high priest or priestess.

is known about the Minoans' educational system, literacy rates, and justice system, for instance. And scholars know either nothing or extremely little about their family life; gender status and roles; childbirth and child-rearing practices; political, social, and military customs; and leisure activities. The result is that, to attempt to reconstruct life in the Minoan towns, the experts are forced to do a considerable amount of guesswork based on archaeological evidence that is often quite slim.

Rulers and High Officials

One important area for which evidence is very patchy is the political and social hierarchy (ladder of social status and authority) in Minoan society. As Rodney Castleden points out, "It is still very difficult to reconstruct" the leaders and social classes

DID THE MINOANS HAVE A KING?

Experts on ancient Crete differ on who ruled Knossos and the other palace-centers during various Minoan periods. In this excerpt from an article in the journal *Athena Review*, scholar Jan Driessen argues that the Minoans had no formal, traditional-style kings before the Mycenaeans took over Crete.

What kind of state did the Minoans develop and cherish before mainland Mycenaeans established themselves on the island after about 1500 B.C. bringing with them a hereditary kingship known as the "wanax," a word still used by Homer some 750 years later? From the start, [Arthur] Evans believed that Knossos was governed by a Priest-King. In the first volume of *The Palace of Minos*, he . . . imagined the ruler seated in the Throne Room flanked by the fresco of griffins. . . . The truth is that we still do not know who was physically in charge of Minoan society. . . . No figural representations of, or textual references to, specific rulers exist, nor are there any explicit references to ruling dynasties. . . . [There is also] the absence of royal or princely graves. . . . We have such "royal" tombs where the Greek Mainland, the Near East, and Mycenaean Crete are concerned, but we lack them on Minoan Crete until after the [Minoans were already in serious decline]. Given the evidence from cemeteries all over the island, it seems that, from Early Minoan times onwards, group burial was the common practice, and even if an individual received more attention through coffin burial or offerings, this happened within the confines of the group. . . . I believe . . . that the absence of princely burials is very difficult to reconcile with the presence of a conjectured powerful ruler.

of Minoan "society with any confidence." The tablets found in the palace-centers, he says, offer only "fleeting glimpses of deities, officials, and bureaucrats," and mostly just "from the fourteenth century B.C."[21] Therefore, not only are the state officials and social classes mentioned in these writings hard to define, it is possible that they reflect only the situation in that particular era and not earlier periods.

Assuming that these aspects of Minoan society *are* generally representative of life in Crete throughout the second millennium B.C., who, according to the clues discovered to date, was in charge of the Minoan towns and city-states? The ancient myths say that Knossos was ruled by a king named Minos. However, that name may be only a title denoting a high-placed official or leader (like the Egyptian title *pharaoh*). It is important to note that these myths coalesced in Greece's Dark Age (ca. 1100–800 B.C.), when most towns in Greece were ruled by local kinglike chieftains, each called a *basileus*. The early myth tellers may simply have assumed, therefore, that the people of the Age of Heroes were also ruled by kings.

Unfortunately, archaeology has yet to settle this question. A number of references have been found in the Minoan tablets to a person called the *wanax*, a title that seems to have had some kind of royal connotation. However, it is not clear whether he was an all-powerful figure or more of a figurehead. Most scholars presently lean toward the latter possibility. This is partly because evidence suggests that the Minoan priesthood may have overshadowed, or at least significantly limited, the monarch's powers. In addition, the tablets make frequent reference to a high official called the *lawagetas*,

roughly translated as "leader of the people." He apparently administered the palace-center and its economic activities on a daily basis. Castleden sums up the most likely scenario, based on the meager evidence, saying that the *lawagetas* may have been

> a kind of prime minister under the Wanax . . . if the Wanax was a ceremonial figurehead with circumscribed powers [authority limited by law or custom]. There is really too little evidence to go on, but what we have is compatible with a Wanax who was a monarch with very limited secular power, a constitutional monarch who formed a charismatic focus for public ceremony, and a Lawagetas who was the effective secular ruler.[22]

Probably of lower (but perhaps of equal) status with the *lawagetas* was a female official known as the *klawiphoros*, or "key bearer." Exactly what she did is unknown, but some evidence points to a religious role, which means she may have been a high priestess. (The references to the key bearer come from Pylos, in the southern mainland. This was a Mycenaean site, but in the fourteenth century B.C. Crete was under Mycenaean control; and in any case, it appears that the Minoans and the mainlanders shared many political and religious titles and customs. Like Knossos, Pylos had a *wanax* and *lawagetas*, so it stands to reason that Knossos, too, had a key bearer.)

In addition, smaller towns in Crete seem to have been run by local mayorlike officials. In the tablets, they bear the title *qa-si-re-wi-ja*, which most scholars believe is "*guasileus*," an early form of the word *basileus*. If this is indeed the case, it neatly

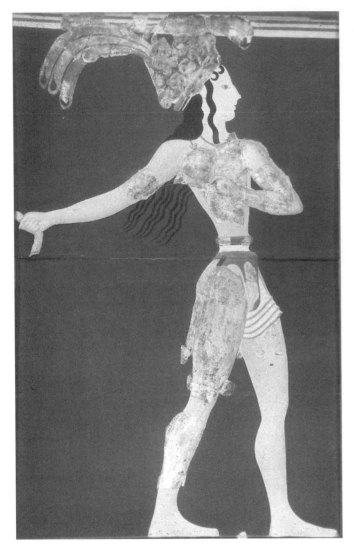

The famous Priest-King Fresco, from Knossos. The impressive figure, whose identity is unknown, wears a crown of lilies and peacock plumes.

Minoans are unclear at best. This is mainly because, as noted scholar Sarah B. Pomeroy points out, "the thousands of ordinary farmers and crafts workers have left almost no trace in the archaeological record."[23] One possible clue comes from Cretan society in the Classical Age (ca. 500–323 B.C.). In his important study of ancient Crete, scholar R.F. Willetts recalls that the common people in classical Crete broke down into three general groups —free citizens, serfs (indentured agricultural workers) with limited civic rights, and serfs with no civic rights (basically slaves). He suggests that this social hierarchy may have been inherited from the Minoans. This is certainly possible, perhaps even probable, but no compelling proof for it has yet been found.

What is more certain, based on the large size and complexity of the Minoan towns, their inhabitants worked hard to build and maintain them and to support the palace-centered economies. The following assessment by Pomeroy explains why they did so, despite the fact that a huge gap in wealth and privilege separated the rulers from the bulk of the population:

In all probability, ordinary Cretan people, like the common people in Egypt and in the Near East, accepted their roles as exploited subjects will-

explains why the rulers of Greek towns in the Dark Age came to use that title.

Commoners and Slaves

As for the people these officials ruled, the societal classes and social status of average

BLACK AFRICANS IN THE MINOAN ISLANDS?

Three representations of black Africans have been found in Minoan paintings. The best known is the so-called Captain of the Blacks Fresco (so named by Arthur Evans), unearthed at Knossos. It shows a Minoan soldier, the "captain," presumably leading one or more black men somewhere, although some scholars have conjectured that the captain is drilling the other men. One theory is that these blacks were mercenaries (paid troops) who made it to Crete on Minoan or Egyptian ships. Another hypothesis suggests they were slaves traded to the Minoans by the Egyptians. The second representation of a black African is a bead representing an African's head on a necklace depicted in a fresco from the Knossos palace-center. The third is a painting found at Thera that shows a black African man standing beside a palm tree. There is no evidence that he actually visited the island, or Crete for that matter, since his likeness might be simply an artistic rendering of black Nubians seen by Minoans who had visited Egypt. On the other hand, he might have been a mercenary, a slave, or simply a visitor to the Minoan islands.

ingly, in the belief that the rigidly hierarchical arrangement was quite proper. It is true that people received benefit [from the rulers] in the form of protection from famine and from outside aggressors. Still, their willing acceptance of the heavy interference in their lives by the [palace-]center indicates something more—their positive identification with the center, that is, the king. . . . He was the embodiment of the state . . . and, most important, the representative of the land and people to the gods. . . . Certainly the kings of ancient Egypt and the Near East derived much of their legitimacy from the official equation of royal power with the will of the gods.[24]

The willing subjects described in this passage were presumably free citizens. Whether Willetts's threefold breakdown for Minoan commoners is accurate, the archaeological evidence indicates that some free Minoans, and probably the central administration and priesthood, too, owned slaves. The inventory lists on the Knossos tablets include at least four references to people being bought. Also, some fragments of a fresco from the palace show a white Minoan officer overseeing what appear to be one or more black African men. (Scholars call it the Captain of the Blacks Fresco.) No black-skinned people were native to ancient Crete. So who were these men? One theory is that they were mercenary (hired) soldiers, and another proposes that they were Nubian slaves traded to the Minoans by the Egyptians (who had conquered Nubia, a land lying south of Egypt). If they were slaves, it should be kept in mind that slavery in ancient Crete, as in other ancient realms, was not generally predicated on racial grounds, as it was in the United States before the Civil War. Ancient slaves were mainly war captives and merchandise to be bought and sold and came in all colors and from all ethnic backgrounds.

Depictions of Minoan Women

Some limited but intriguing evidence has been found for the status of another crucial segment of Minoan society—women. Many of the wall paintings and carved scenes on seals found in the Cretan palace-centers, as well as in towns such as Akrotiri on Thera, contain prominent representations of women. The Naval Festival Fresco from Akrotiri and the Grandstand Fresco and Sacred Dance Fresco from Knossos, among others, show dominant female figures who were probably priestesses.

On a more secular level, the Ladies in Blue Fresco, unearthed by Arthur Evans at Knossos, shows three young women, seemingly wives or daughters of palace-center officials. The ladies are sitting and gossiping about

The Ladies in Blue Fresco, found by Sir Arthur Evans at Knossos, shows some fashionable young women wearing elegant outfits and a great deal of jewelry.

This illustration of young Minoan women, from an early twentieth-century book about ancient Cretan myths, was based in part on the Ladies in Blue Fresco.

some sort of entertainment they are watching. "Wearing elaborate [dresses], open in front to reveal their breasts," says Edey, and

festooned with necklaces and bracelets, their hair curled and freighted with ropes of beads, they make a charming group. Their heads are turned this

way and that as they talk, their hands fluttering in the most elegant and refined gestures imaginable.[25]

The ladies in this and similar examples of Minoan art are more than just colorful and charming. Their elegant costumes, partial nudity (which their husbands and fathers apparently condoned), and carefree demeanor create a markedly different image than the more conservative and somber depictions of women in Greek art in later ages. These Minoan works bespeak a high level of respect for women. "No society that did not admire women and give them a great deal of freedom," Edey remarks, "could possibly have created such works."[26] Willetts agrees, writing that the frescoes in question

> bear witness to the prominence of women in Minoan society. . . . Women are painted on a larger scale than anyone else and with elaborate detail. Women in the crowd are on the same scale as the men, indicating that it was not their sex but their function that made the larger-scale ladies so special.[27]

Unfortunately, these images from Minoan art do not tell us much more than that some Minoan women were highly regarded and enjoyed an unusual amount of status and perhaps freedom of movement and expression. No evidence, artistic or otherwise, suggests that women held positions of political power (with the possible exception of the key bearers, whose functions and powers are uncertain). It is also unclear whether the high female status depicted in these artworks existed among the lower classes as well. It is possible that only women from wealthy, noble families had such status.

Dress Styles and Makeup

Much clearer, thanks to a number of archaeological finds, are the dress styles, hairstyles, and personal hygiene of Minoan women (and men, too). Here, care must be taken not to misinterpret the renderings of women's costumes in the art uncovered from the palace-centers. The Ladies in Blue Fresco and other paintings, as well as several exquisite ceramic figurines, show women wearing long, elegant dresses with the fronts open to expose their breasts. In the early decades of Minoan research, most scholars jumped to the conclusion that most or all young Minoan women dressed this way. However, the consensus today is that the art found in the palaces was mostly religious in nature. And as Castleden puts it, "If such representations are seen as religious art and the women are seen as priestesses, temple attendants, dancers, or even goddesses . . . it may well be that women uncovered their breasts only during acts of religious worship."[28]

Indeed, the general physical appearance of the Minoans in their art is probably largely selective and representational. Most people depicted, both male and female, are thin, muscular, tanned, and attractive, with long wavy black hair falling to their shoulders and sometimes to their waists. It is highly unlikely that all Minoans looked like ballet dancers and matadors, as these artworks would suggest. But such ideal depictions are not surprising because they have been a regular feature of the art of most human cultures, including today's. A majority of the models and actors who populate modern soap operas, movies, and television and magazine ads are far more fit and attractive than the average person.

Still, the women's fashions shown in the palace paintings and sculptures must have reflected to some degree the general dress styles and outfits of the day, at least the formal wear. The longer dresses, almost always ankle length, accentuated the hips and breasts and drew tightly in at the waists.

This detail from the Procession Fresco, found at Knossos, shows Minoan women wearing long, elegant dresses of layered fabric.

The tops of the dresses often had short, tight sleeves and ruffled bodices with an open slit running from the neck down to the navel. If the theory that exposing the breasts was uncommon and somehow ceremonial is correct, the average woman kept the slit closed enough to cover the nipples and showed only the amount of cleavage seen in many modern party dresses. The skirt sections of these dresses had several overlapping layers, each made of cloth of a different color or fabric (producing a kind of checkered pattern).

Once more, such elaborate dresses may have been reserved for religious worship, public festivals, and other special occasions. It is unclear what ordinary women who lived in the Minoan towns wore on a daily basis. Perhaps they donned dresses similar in style to those in the paintings but less fancy and looser fitting to allow them freer movement for everyday tasks. Or they may have worn comfortable undergarments covered by informal, flowing outer cloaks (called himations), as many classical Greek women did.

THE GIRL WITH BRIGHT LIPS

In this excerpt from his book *The Civilization of Ancient Crete*, scholar R.F. Willetts describes the setting and larger context of the famous "La Parisienne" figure from a fresco found at Knossos.

The female figure known as "La Parisienne" belongs to a larger composition known as the Camp Stool Fresco, consisting of pairs of young persons in long robes, seated facing each other and passing a goblet. The girl, with bright lips, expressive eye, perky nose, and elegant hair curling down over her brow, received her name [which compares her to women depicted in nineteenth-century French art] when she was discovered. It is not inept and also suggests the impressionistic [sketchy] style of her representation. . . . The composition adorned an upper room in the northwest corner of the Palace of Knossos at the time of its destruction. Since [she] was one of a pair of twin figures considerably larger than the rest, it has been inferred that these represented a pair of goddesses [or priestesses] presiding over religious rites.

The Minoan lady dubbed "La Parisienne" wears heavy lipstick and eyeliner.

Whatever their attire, Minoan women appear to have worn makeup (although, again, this may have been restricted to priestesses, court ladies, and/or ordinary women only on special occasions). One of the most famous frescoes discovered at Knossos—which scholars dubbed La Parisienne—shows a woman (in profile), probably a priestess, wearing heavy makeup. Her eyelids and eyebrow are enlarged and darkened, indicating some sort of mascara; and her lips are painted bright red. To put on their makeup, Minoan ladies used mirrors of polished bronze. And for their hair they used combs, at first made of wood, but after about 1500 B.C. made of ivory.

Men's Dress Styles and Professions

Both men and women in Minoan Crete wore jewelry, including hairpins, earrings, necklaces, pendants, bracelets, anklets, and rings. These appear frequently in art, and some actual examples have been found in tombs and ruined houses. Unlike women, however, men generally wore less elaborate outfits that left more of the body exposed. In the Early and Middle Minoan periods, it appears that most or all men wore loin-cloths, sometimes held in place by a belt. Some artistic representations show loin-cloths that wrapped around the thighs separately. In others, the loincloths wrapped around the hips like a short skirt. Over time, this kilt-like arrangement evolved into shorts similar to those worn today. An archer depicted on a jar found at Knossos wears shorts having two layers, similar to the layers in women's dresses. Minoan men also donned codpieces, which covered the genitals. These were worn both over and in-stead of loincloths, and after about 1700 B.C. they became increasingly exaggerated in size and decoration, like those worn in Italy during the Renaissance.

Another section of the Procession Fresco shows several men serving a woman who may be a high priestess. The men wear kilt-like outfits and armbands.

Judging by paintings and other artworks, Minoan men seem to have worn little else besides their kilts, shorts, and codpieces. Sometimes they are shown wearing sandals or boots, and also hats (to protect them from the hot Mediterranean sun), which were usually flat at the top and had thick rolled brims. But though the men are most often shown with bare chests and legs, it is likely that they wore simple cloaks or shawls on cool days and in the cooler evening hours.

It should be emphasized that the outfits men wore likely depended to some degree on their professions or principal activities. Some evidence suggests, for instance, that farmers and herders sometimes wore cloaks or tunics made from animals skins; this would make sense considering that they worked closely with animals of various kinds. And judging from evidence from some Mycenaean sites, at least some of the soldiers of that era probably wore some kind of armor, either of leather, metal, or a mixture of the two.

Farming, herding, and soldiering were not the only activities that men engaged in.

In the towns, Evans and other archaeologists found evidence for many different kinds of craftsmen, including potters, metalsmiths, stonecutters, ivory workers, and seal makers. There were also fishermen, rowers for the fleets, traders, priests, palace guards, and scribes. Meanwhile, construction and maintenance jobs in the towns were likely performed by a mixture of slaves and free men. It is unknown whether the free men who worked for the state were paid. Because no money existed, their compensation probably consisted of extra rations and/or luxury goods from the palace collectives.

The details of the lives of these workers are unknown. But keep in mind that most of the huge town that once surrounded the Knossos palace-center still lies buried and unexcavated. And the remains of previously unknown Minoan towns continue to be discovered from time to time. Archaeologists and other scholars are hopeful that a great deal about life in these towns will be learned in the years to come.

CHAPTER FOUR

MINOAN PAINTING, ARCHITECTURE, CRAFTS, AND WRITING

When approaching the topic of the Minoans' creative output, archaeologists are fortunately on firmer ground than they are with Minoan political and social customs and habits. Although most evidence for the latter has disappeared (or remains undiscovered), surviving examples of Minoan architecture, painting, and crafts are fairly numerous and are often extremely vivid and evocative. They are also quite original and distinctive. Excavators and historians have frequently noted that the Minoans borrowed many of their creative styles and artistic ideas from the older civilizations of the Near East, especially Egypt. Yet they did not simply copy these ideas; rather, they absorbed them, rethought them, and then applied them in new ways. Sarah Pomeroy explains it this way:

The Cretans developed extensive commercial and diplomatic relations with the states along the Syrian and Phoenician coasts, and they adopted both the techniques and styles of the older civilizations. The spirit of Minoan art and architecture, however, was very different. The predominant function of palace art in the East was to glorify the royal household. The

kings were depicted as mighty conquerors and powerful rulers. In Minoan art, on the other hand, there are no scenes that show the king as a conquering warrior and indeed very few, if any, images of royal pomp.[29]

Instead, Minoan artists produced mostly scenes of normal people and animals in everyday settings, not only the palace-centers but also the countryside. Though the scenes depicted are often casual, at times even playful, there seems to be a religious theme or aspect in most of them. Such underlying themes are often not very obvious to the modern eye, but they would have been perfectly plain to the average Minoan. Also, for him or her art was not meant simply as a form of decoration or an expression of the artist's personal feelings. It was more ritualistic in nature—an expression of *society's* feelings, which emphasized the importance of maintaining community traditions and standards. As noted classical scholar Nanno Marinatos puts it:

The relationship between art and the viewer was very different in the Bronze Age. . . . For a Minoan . . . a painting represented part of his tradition, which was comprehensible and

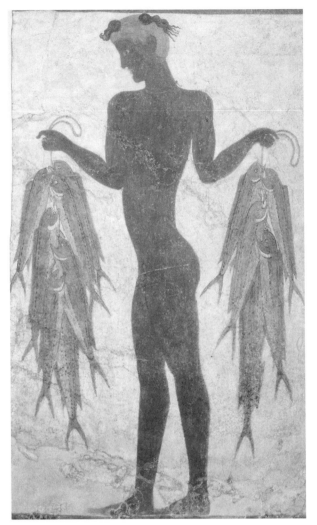

The fresco showing the "young fisherman" (as scholars often call him), who carries his day's catch, was discovered at Akrotiri, on Thera.

What is more, by closely examining Minoan creative output, scholars can detect hints of the Minoan character that elude them in the more poorly documented political and social realms. "It is clear," Rodney Castleden observes, "that the Minoans developed [their] art in a way that was strongly characteristic of their personality . . . to such an extent that we get, even from fragments of artifacts, a strong sense of the Minoans' personality."[31]

Regrettably, the remnants of another aspect of Minoan creativity— writing—are a good deal less revealing. Large numbers of tablets and inscriptions remain undeciphered to this day. Yet, by applying ingenuity and years of hard work, by the mid-twentieth century a handful of scholars had learned how to translate a significant portion of them.

Architectural Styles and Features

Before any Minoan writings, paintings, or figurines were discovered, the Minoans were initially revealed to the modern world through their architecture. After all, the first remnants uncovered of that enigmatic vanished people were the foundations, walls, and staircases of the magnificent palace-center at Knossos. The structure is so large and complex that, even if it was the only Minoan building ever unearthed, much could be learned from it about those who erected it.

Fortunately, it is by no means the only building of its kind known. Since Arthur Evans's initial excavations in 1900, the

even predictable. It can be said that art was a representation of the collective values of the society of which the viewer was a member. Thus, the relationship between art and the viewer was intimate and the function of the painting important.[30]

number of palace-centers unearthed has continued to grow. Besides the Knossos complex, the ones at Phaistos, Mallia, and Kato Zakro remain the principal large-scale versions that are fully excavated. However, some previously unknown palace-centers have been recently discovered, and archaeologists are hard at work at bringing them to light. One, first recognized in 1985, is at Petras, on the northeastern coast of Crete. Another, discovered in 1991, is at Galatas, fewer than twenty miles south of Knossos. And still another was found more recently beneath the houses and streets of the busy city of Khania in northwestern Crete. (Un-

fortunately, the existence of these modern structures, most of which cannot be removed, severely limits and slows the efforts of archaeologists at the Khania site.)

All of these palace-centers seem to have originally had the same basic architectural features, which were often quite distinctive from those exhibited in the palaces of Egypt and Mesopotamia. First, the Minoan versions all covered extremely large areas of ground and featured complex, rambling, sometimes multistoried, and often split-level clusters of rooms. A Dartmouth College team of experts led by classicist Jeremy B. Rutter recently made the following useful

A portion of the ruins of the palace-center at Phaistos, in southern Crete, one of the first and largest of the Minoan palaces unearthed in modern times.

general observations about the complicated layout of the Knossos palace-center:

> The architecture of the palace is arranged in an irregularly stepped series of projecting rectangular masses resembling a compactly arranged pile of cardboard boxes of different sizes. This irregular contouring of the palace's exterior is true both of its plan . . . and of its elevation [vertical components], which would have featured flat roofs at a wide variety of distinct levels interrupted irregularly by the unroofed spaces over courts and lightwells. The sheer bulk of the building . . . coupled with the irregularity of its exterior surfaces, would have made it difficult for the visitor to obtain a quick impression of its true size. Rather . . . a prehistoric islander or mainlander who was not

This reconstruction shows a cutaway section of the Knossos palace that captures the tremendous complexity of the layout.

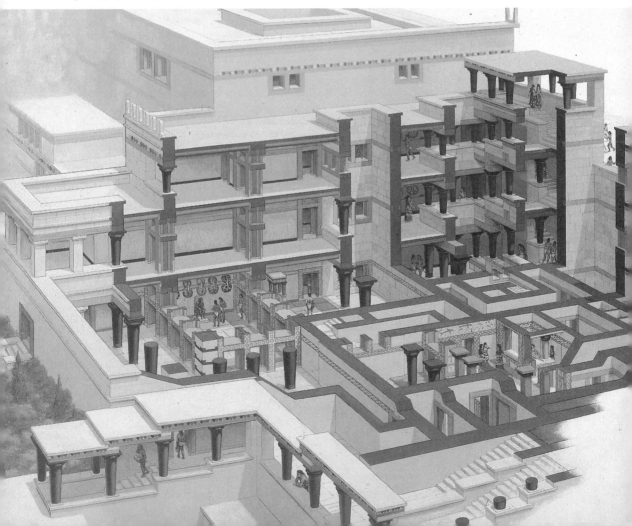

used to seeing large-scale settlement architecture of any kind, would have perceived the building as having no borders, as being virtually limitless.[32]

It is thus easy to see how the legends of the mazelike Labyrinth originated.

Another distinct architectural feature of the Minoan palaces was dubbed the "lustral basin" by Arthur Evans. These are tiny rooms or spaces (usually squares no more than four or five feet on a side) located at the bottoms of winding staircases. Leading nowhere, they are an odd sort of architectural cul-de-sac. At first, many scholars thought these spaces were ritual bathing areas. But the more recent and prevailing interpretation is that they were private sanctuaries where priests and priestesses conducted hidden rituals.

Still another feature that makes Minoan architecture different than that of other ancient cultures, one that immediately catches the eye and makes a lasting impression, is the shape and color of the pillars. First, these columns (which were made of wood) tapered downward, unlike Greco-Roman and other ancient versions, which had no observable taper. Also, the Minoan columns were painted bright red or black. "The most likely explanation for the downward taper," says Evans's recent biographer, Sylvia L. Horwitz,

> was that the tree trunks used in ancient times were unseasoned [fresh] and the best way to keep unseasoned timber from sprouting was to plant it upside-down. The Minoans had painted their graceful columns either red or black, with the capitals [tops] made wide enough to throw rainwater clear of the base, which might otherwise rot.[33]

The Minoan Frescoes

Next to the architecture of the palace-centers, perhaps the most visually stunning examples of Minoan creativity are the many painted frescoes discovered at Knossos and other sites. These were not features merely of the palaces. A number have been found in private residences, including the so-called House of the Frescoes, lying northwest of the Knossos palace. In the second volume of his masterly *Palace of Minos at Knossos*, Evans gave this enthusiastic description of the unexpectedly high level of luxury these paintings imparted to what was quite an average home:

> The house itself was quite a small one. . . . Yet the citizen, we may suppose, of the petty burgher [upper middle] class who had his habitation here, is shown by the remains that have come down to us—a mere fraction of the whole—to have been a man of cultivated taste. The painted decoration of the walls is unrivaled of its kind for its picturesque setting, and the many-colored effect is enhanced, not only by the varied choice of flowers, but the convention of the rocks cut like agates to show their brilliant veins.[34]

The majority of the Minoan frescoes discovered so far existed in broken fragments when archaeologists first unearthed them. Yet even in their fragmentary state, they revealed tantalizing glimpses of Minoan men and women engaged in activities evidently characteristic of their culture. Following is Evans's description, penned in 1900 during his first months at Knossos, of what he could see on the pieces of a fresco showing crowds of people watching public spectacles:

EXCAVATING A PALACE BURIED BENEATH A MODERN CITY

One serious difficulty that archaeologists often face in today's increasingly urbanized world is finding important remains of vanished civilizations beneath the streets and residential districts of busy cities. Residents and authorities are often reluctant to allow their dwellings and roads to be demolished in the name of science, as the archaeologists trying to extricate a new Minoan palace-center at Khania, in western Crete, have learned. In 2003 an interviewer for the scholarly journal *Athena Review* asked the leader of the expedition, Maria Andreadaki-Vlasaki, to comment on the problems encountered thus far by the excavators. "It is really very difficult to conduct rescue and even systematic excavations in the center of a vibrant town, like the modern town of Khania," she answered.

> Another difficulty of the excavations is the big number of different layers of earth created during the 5,000 years of habitation in the same area. . . . Soon, a huge cover will be erected . . . to protect the Greek-Swedish excavations. . . . Another ambitious project, not being fulfilled for the moment, is the uncovering of . . . part of [an] important [religious] sanctuary. . . . The study is ready, but this work will cause a serious change in the [traffic] circulation in the town, since [the street lying above the ruins] is an arterial road, and the local authorities are not ready to risk it.

At a glance we recognize court ladies in elaborate [attire]. . . . In the best executed pieces these . . . ladies are seated in groups with their legs half bent under them, engaged in animated conversation emphasized by expressive gesticulation [hand gestures]. . . . The men, none of whom are bearded, are naked except for [a] loincloth and footgear with banded . . . continuations above the ankle, resembling the buckskins worn by the warriors on the fresco fragments from Mycenae. . . . These unique representations of crowds of men and women within the walls and towns and palaces supply a new and striking commentary on the familiar passage of Homer describing the ancient populousness of the Cretan cities.[35]

Features and Techniques of Minoan Painting

This painting and the others Evans discovered in the years that followed were eventually painstakingly restored. Together with the frescoes found elsewhere, particularly the stunning examples unearthed at Akrotiri, on Thera, beginning in the late 1960s, they demonstrate certain general standard characteristics of Minoan wall painting. The Dartmouth team here summarizes some of the main ones:

> Specific skin color conventions exist for the sexes, probably adopted from Egyptian wall painting . . . red for male, white for female. . . . There are no . . . historical or mythological [scenes]. Scenes from nature are realistic in terms of the movements of animal or human participants. The artists were keen observers of action. Likewise, flowers and birds are portrayed "naturalistically," although specialists knowledgeable in the fields of botany and ornithology have often shown that the plants and animals in question have no true counterpart in nature but merely *appear* to be represented accurately. . . . There is no attempt to indicate depth by means of perspective or diminution of figure scale with distance. The range of colors is remarkably varied. There is a comparatively wide variety of scenes and individual motifs in Minoan painting as a whole.

A fresco found at Hagia Triada shows a religious procession, probably leading up to a sacrifice. The people and animals are portrayed realistically.

. . . [Also, there is an] absence of hunting scenes and scenes of warfare in [Minoan art].[36]

How did Minoan artists, working nearly a thousand years before the golden age of classical Greece, create these murals, which in beauty and skill of execution rival those of the greatest artists of later cultures? "The technique for producing the Minoan frescos varied," Castleden explains.

Some were frescos in the truest sense. Colors were applied to wet plaster and left to sink into it as the plaster dried. Others were painted onto a dry plaster surface. Still others were pro-

duced by means of a curious inlay technique. After the initial fresco painting had dried, some areas requiring more detailed work were cut away, and refilled and recolored with fresh wet plaster.[37]

The Importance of Pottery

The artisans who produced the Minoan crafts achieved results nearly as striking as those of the painters. Evidence shows that craft workshops existed in both the countryside and towns in the early Minoan centuries. A potter's workshop was discovered in the tiny rural village of Myrtos, for example. As the towns grew in size and the palace-

These exquisite examples of Minoan pottery are on display at the archaeological museum at Heraklion (near Knossos), Crete's major modern city.

centers gained nearly complete control of society, however, most craftspeople congregated in the urban areas. In fact, workshops were often set up right inside the palace complexes; this suggests that the central authority exercised tight control over craft production to make it easier to redistribute the goods locally or to use them in foreign trade.

Other evidence shows that in many cases the items made by the craftspeople increased markedly in quality as the towns grew and the urban workshops prospered. Take the example of potters. Before the Middle Minoan (or First Palace) Period, most Minoan pottery was fashioned either without pottery wheels or with rudimentary ones that turned very slowly. And the ceramic objects were then hardened in an ordinary fire. In the improved process in the urban workshops, a faster wheel came into use and stone kilns, which produced higher temperatures, replaced open fires. These advances produced more even and predictable results and allowed the potters to turn out items of more varied shapes and more delicate construction.

Surviving pottery is very telling about Minoan civilization in two ways. First, the kinds of ceramic items found—cups, goblets, bowls, pitchers, teapots, frying pans, strainers, storage jars, and so forth—reveal some of the people's domestic habits and practices. Second, the remains of these pots, which underwent steady changes in style and technique over time, allow archaeologists to date various stages of Minoan civilization, or at least track important changes in it. "As fast as the pots were damaged or broken, they were thrown out," writes Maitland Edey about ancient pottery in general.

But the smashed bits—or shards— were as hard as rock and accumulated rapidly under earthen floors or on town rubbish heaps. As a result, every ancient archaeological site contains masses of them. When a site is excavated, shards are collected and a careful record is made of the different levels at which they are found. This done, an expert can reconstruct a cultural sequence for a given place by noting the changes in shape and in ornamentation [of the pots] as the site is worked more deeply and thus backward in time. . . . This technique has enabled archaeologists to sort out various stages or cultural developments in the Aegean . . . revealing not only what was going on culturally in various places, but the order in which events happened.[38]

Other Crafts

In addition to exquisite pottery, Minoan artisans turned out finely made examples of stoneware, metalware of many types, and various items of shell, bone, and ivory. Stone vases, bowls, jars, and so forth were likely initially inspired by Egyptian versions; but Minoan artisans developed the art to new heights. These vessels were fashioned from a wide variety of stones, especially harder ones, which often have more color and finer textures. These included alabaster, gypsum, serpentine, obsidian, limestone, and marble, among others. The basic technique was first to find or cut a chunk of stone of the desired size and slowly chip away small pieces on the outer edges until the outside shape was established. Then the artisan hollowed out the center using a

This magnificent twelve-inch-high bull's head found at Knossos was carved from steatite (or soapstone). Its eyes are red jasper and its horns goldplated.

hand-turned drill made of bronze or wood and/or a hammer and chisel. Finally, a coarse lump of stone was used to smooth the inner and outer surface, and the vessel was polished.

Meanwhile, Minoan metalworkers produced copper, bronze, gold, and silver items of fine quality. Bronze (and for some items occasionally copper) was employed in making cooking pots, bowls, storage jars, tools, eating utensils, swords, armor, figurines, and much more. Gold and silver were used to make drinking cups for the well-to-do or for the temples, as well as jewelry and decorative inlays on other materials, such as wooden chests and stone bowls.

Most metal items were made by hammering and cutting the metal into the desired shape. But some solid bronze items were cast using a method experts call *cire perdue*. A figurine, for example, was first fashioned in wax. The artisan then encased it in clay, which hardened, and poured molten bronze in through a small hole in the clay. The hot metal melted the wax and displaced it, and when the metal solidified, the clay was removed, exposing the finished figurine.

Shell and ivory were used to decorate wooden chests and other furniture. Game boards and pieces were also made of ivory. A beautiful ivory game board (which might, alternatively, have been used in religious rituals) was found in the ruins of the Knossos palace-center. The ivory was further decorated with small quantities of gold, silver, and crystal. Ivory was also employed in making figurines and plaques. One of the most-often photographed of these figurines, depicting a snake goddess, was also discovered at Knossos.

Minoan Scribes and Written Scripts

Painters and craftspeople were not the only highly skilled individuals who worked in and around the palace-centers. There were also a great many scribes, who specialized in keeping inventories and other records. Based on evidence from the surviving tablets, experts estimate that as many seventy scribes were working in the Knossos palace alone circa 1380 B.C. This is not surprising considering the enormous volume of goods and materials collected and stored in these facilities, all of which had to be kept track of as they came in and went out.

Generally speaking, it appears that the palace scribes utilized three different kinds of written scripts over the course of the Minoan centuries. The first, which appeared around 2100 B.C., was pictographic (or hieroglyphic). This means that it consisted of little images, or hieroglyphs, of plants, wheels, axes, people, animals, and so forth. This script remains largely undeciphered, but scholars believe that some of the signs stand for ideas, and others are syllabic, meaning that they represent spoken syllables.

By the 1700s B.C., the Minoans had adopted another kind of script, which Evans named Linear A. Apparently mostly syllabic, it contains about seventy characters, some of them pictographic, and the rest shaped more like letters. Most of the Linear A tablets discovered at Knossos and other sites were found beside others bearing writing in the third script, which Evans called Linear B. (Linear B tablets have also been found at numerous Mycenaean sites on the mainland.) It appears that this script came into use in Crete sometime during the 1400s B.C.

This tablet discovered at the Knossos palace-center bears an inscription in Linear A characters. Linear A has not yet been deciphered.

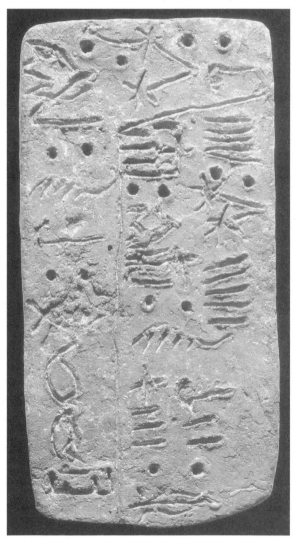

MICHAEL VENTRIS DECIPHERS LINEAR B

In this excerpt from his book *The Greek Achievement*, popular scholar Charles Freeman provides this account of how Michael Ventris deciphered Linear B and proved it was an early form of Greek.

> He did not expect, at first, to find that Linear B was Greek; some relationship to Etruscan was his first guess. . . . The real step forward came when he tried to fit the names of Cretan cities—Knossos; its harbor, Amnisos; and another local town . . . which he assumed might have remained unchanged over the centuries, with syllables from Linear B. He began to get some matches . . . and thus some syllabic sounds which he could use in other contexts. An exciting moment came when the sounds *ko-wo* and *ko-we*, the *kouros* (boy) and *kore* (girl) of Homer's Greek (the earliest Greek texts to have survived) emerged. The Homeric words for *shepherd, bronzesmith*, and *goldsmith* were similarly deciphered. . . . As remaining texts were unraveled . . . names of Greek gods emerged, among them Poseidon, Zeus, and Athena. . . . The discovery established for Greek the longest continuous history of any European language which survives today and a language which has fed into others.

These Linear B characters, which appear on a tablet found at Pylos, in southern Greece, are an early form of Greek.

Evans and his contemporaries were unable to decipher Linear A and B and assumed they were both written forms of the long-dead, and presumably non-Greek, Minoan and Mycenaean languages. In 1952, however, British scholar Michael Ventris managed to decipher much of Linear B. The scholarly world was both shocked and delighted to learn that it was an early form of Greek, which proved that the Mycenaeans were the direct predecessors of the classical Greeks. Linear A still defies translation. But the scholarly consensus is that it is a crude form of the non-Greek Minoan language and that the Mycenaeans adopted it to their own tongue, altering it somewhat in the process and thereby producing Linear B.

The discovery of the Linear A and B scripts revealed to Evans and other early experts on Aegean civilization that the Minoans, at least the scribes and perhaps a handful of others, were literate. But the nature of these scripts and the distribution of the tablets on which they were written raised new questions and mysteries for these scholars. Why did Linear B suddenly come into use in Crete during the 1400s B.C.? And why did the Linear B tablets subsequently outnumber the Linear A tablets at Knossos by a factor of ten to one? It took several decades of further discovery and research to show how these developments were connected to the relationship between the Mycenaeans and the Minoans, a turbulent one in which, it appears, one culture eventually subjugated the other.

CHAPTER FIVE

MINOAN RELIGIOUS PLACES, GODS, AND RITUALS

Based on the surviving evidence, there is no doubt that the Minoans were a highly religious people. Belief in and worship of divine beings appears to have permeated their lives on nearly every level and to a degree that the average person today might find bewildering or disconcerting. In fact, it would probably not be an exaggeration to say that religion was the single-most important aspect of Minoan life and culture.

Unfortunately for modern observers, though, the Linear A tablets, which contain the only-known written version of the long-dead Minoan language, remain largely undeciphered. Consequently, no textual evidence for Minoan religion has survived. Imagine archaeologists of the far future attempting to understand the Christian religion practiced today (assuming that the present civilization has passed away by that time) but lacking a single line from the Bible, any other Christian religious writings, or any commentaries and descriptions of them!

Another problem is that Linear A was likely used in the same way as Linear B—almost exclusively for keeping inventories of goods. Thus, "even if Linear A were deciphered," the members of the Dartmouth College archaeological team point out, "it is unlikely that much information regarding Minoan cult [religious] practices, much less Minoan religious ideology, would be forthcoming above and beyond the names of the divinities which the Minoans worshipped."[39]

It is therefore extremely difficult for modern researchers to understand the exact beliefs, rituals, and practices of Minoan religion. And archaeologists and other scholars are forced to piece together a very speculative picture of that ancient faith based on a wide range of scattered, often disconnected archaeological clues. Before any tentative attempt to describe the actual rituals of the faith, it is necessary first to describe these clues. They can conveniently be grouped into general categories, including places of worship, gods, and religious symbols and sacred animals.

Places of Worship— Cave Sanctuaries

One reason why modern scholarly opinion holds that religion was so important to the Minoans is that their places of worship were nearly everywhere. They had shrines or sanctuaries (sacred areas) in caves, on mountaintops, on roadsides, within the palace-centers, and likely in private homes as well. The exact religious functions of each of these places are unclear, partly because the evidence remains scattered and sketchy. (For example, though many cave sanctuaries are known, none have yet been completely excavated and documented.) But it seems probable that all such places, regardless of how and how often they were used, were equally sacred in the Minoan mind.

Looking at the Minoan cave sanctuaries first, archaeological evidence shows that worship in them during the second millennium B.C. was likely an extension of earlier uses for caves. Examination of artifacts from accumulated layers on cave floors indicates that people lived in caves on Crete during the Stone Age. After they moved out and began living in houses in villages (perhaps in the fourth millennium B.C.), the caves became cemeteries. Finally, about 2200 to 2000 B.C., when the palace-centers began to

be built, many of these same caves were converted to cult sites where people gathered to worship. Proof takes the form of bones of sacrificed animals and other cult artifacts in the cave-floor deposits, all initially dating from that era.

Thus, the desire to follow ancient tradition is undoubtedly one reason why worship often took place in caves. But it is likely that the unusual physical conditions of caves played a role, too. Rodney Castleden has suggested that caves were used for worship and burial partly

because of their mysterious and otherworldly atmosphere. One has only to descend into the magnificent caverns of Psychro (south of Mallia) or Skotino (east of Knossos) to sense the awe

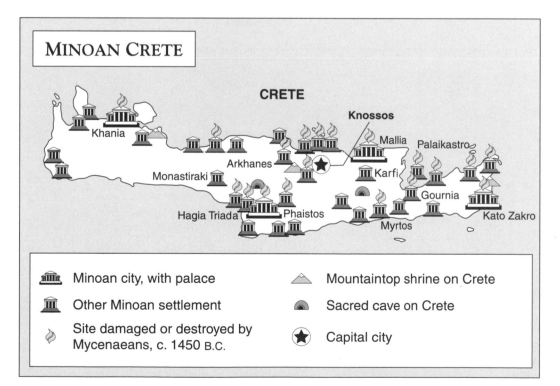

MINOAN CRETE

CRETE

Knossos

Khania

Mallia   Palaikastro

Arkhanes   Karfi

Monastiraki

Gournia

Hagia Triada   Phaistos

Myrtos   Kato Zakro

🏛 Minoan city, with palace

🏛 Other Minoan settlement

🔥 Site damaged or destroyed by Mycenaeans, c. 1450 B.C.

⛰ Mountaintop shrine on Crete

◉ Sacred cave on Crete

★ Capital city

MINOAN THOLOS TOMBS

In very early Minoan times, people buried their dead in caves and rock shelters. Cremation was very rare. Eventually, perhaps by the start of the third millennium B.C., circular communal tombs made of stone became common, as described here by Maitland Edey in this excerpt from his informative study of the Minoans, *Lost World of the Aegean*.

> One of the most remarkable features of Minoan culture is the tholos tomb. Nearly 80 of the low, round stone structures have been discovered, most of them in the Mesara Plain near Phaistos. Their walls are heavy, and they curve inward as they rise, suggesting that they were vaulted. However, since all the roofs have fallen in, it is not possible to tell whether they had true domes or whether they were topped by flat wooden coverings. But it is certain that they were used communally. All seem to have been next to settlements. And most are very old, dating from as early as 2800 B.C. . . . They were used again and again—gradually filled up with skeletons and grave goods, then periodically cleaned out, fumigated, a new earth floor laid down, and the process repeated. Some tholoi were in continuous use for a thousand years.

that the Minoan pilgrims, too, must have felt. They are places apart, like no other, places where deities might yet dwell.[40]

It appears that each of the large towns with palace-centers, and perhaps a number of the smaller towns as well, had sacred caves within walking distance. The main one used by the residents of Knossos was the Skotino cave, which likely drew worshippers from other parts of Crete as well. Indeed, it remains one of the most impressive caves in Crete. It has four separate caverns, the first of which is about 300 feet long, 120 feet wide, and 150 feet high in places. The center of this cathedral-like chamber is dominated by a huge stalagmite that projects upward from the floor. Evidence sug-

gests that the Minoans held such pillarlike formations sacred somehow. Pools of water inside the caves appear also to have been viewed as holy. People from Knossos also visited the smaller cave of Eleuthia, near the port of Amnisos; this cave was likely still used as a sanctuary or cemetery during Greece's Dark Age, as Homer mentions it in the *Odyssey*.

Places of Worship— Peak Sanctuaries

In the physical sense, as well as in the mood they evoked, Minoan peak sanctuaries were almost the exact opposite of the cave versions. The peak sanctuaries were always situated out in the open, on barren, windswept hilltops, ledges, or promontories. Their elevation varied considerably. The lowest found to date rests only about 650 feet above sea level. The highest yet discovered, at Karfi (south of Mallia), sits at nearly 3,600 feet. "Solitary, raised to the skies, exposed to the wind, silent but for the sounds of birds and wild goats," Castleden remarks, "the peaks must have seemed places that were propitious [favorable] for meetings with the gods."[41] In fact, it is almost certain that the Minoans believed that some of

their gods dwelled on mountaintops. This was a common tenet of faith for a majority of the ancient peoples of Europe, Africa, and Asia; another example was the early belief by Greek mainlanders that their gods lived atop Mt. Olympus.

Most or all of these sacred mountaintop sites, which first appeared between 2200 and 2100 B.C., featured shrines constructed in various ways. Perhaps the most common arrangement consisted of a series of flat

The entrance to the Dictean Cave (at the base of Mt. Dikte in Crete). Used by the Minoans, the cave remained sacred in later ages as the supposed birthplace of the god Zeus.

stone terraces on different levels. Each terrace had one or more altar stones. And stone walls lined the outer perimeter of the complex, with tall masts and/or stone representations of bull horns rising from strategic locations on the walls. Two surviving Minoan rhyta (drinking vessels shaped like horns) bear carved scenes showing such sacred enclosures.

In an unknown number of these enclosures actual temples were constructed. The best-known example, and probably the most important to the Minoans, was atop Mt. Juktus, a few miles south of Knossos. The temple inside the enclosure walls was a long, narrow building, probably originally two stories in height, perched near the edge of a steep cliff. The building had five separate chambers, each of which may have held its own shrine or holy area. When in use, these rooms, as well as the outer terraces, were loaded with elaborate furnishings. These included stone tables for sacrificing animals, oil lamps for evening worship, plates and cups for sacred meals, and gifts that pilgrims brought for the gods.

It is unknown when and how often people worshipped at Juktus and places like it in any given year. The Dartmouth team suggests:

> It is quite possible that these peak sanctuaries were visited only on spe-

This stone representation of bull's horns is located on an outer edge of the Knossos palace. Similar symbols were erected at Minoan religious sites.

Beyond these steps, located on the south side of the Minoan palace-center at Gournia, is a sacred area with a stone platform on which animal sacrifices took place.

cial religious holidays, much as similar mountaintop chapels are today in Greece, since in many cases the sanctuaries are too remotely located to have served daily religious purposes.[42]

What seems more certain is that both the Minoans and the Mycenaeans (after they took over Crete) viewed the Juktus complex as special; on the one hand, it was the chief peak sanctuary used by the residents of Knossos, the largest palace-center town; also, it came to be seen as sacred to the Greek god Zeus, originally a Mycenaean deity.

Places of Worship—
Palace-Centers

However special or sacred in its own right, the temple in the Juktus sanctuary was a minor one to the Minoans. Their main shrines appear to have been in the palace-

centers. In fact, in recent years the consensus of scholarly opinion has come to view the palace-centers themselves as huge religious temples. This interpretation does not necessarily negate or conflict with those in which these structures acted as both administrative centers for the collectives and royal residences. The key factor or question is: Who was in charge? If the king, prime minister, and nobles were all priests and the government was a strict theocracy, multiple roles for the palaces, including that of religious center, makes perfect sense. Nanno Marinatos speaks for a majority of scholars when she says:

> Given the great number of sanctuaries [all over Crete] it is difficult to envisage the priesthood as an exclusive caste with a very specialized function in society. Rather, it is possible that

the priests were members of the noble, ruling class; in fact, they may have been identical with the ruling class. . . . I believe that the priestly class and the nobility were one and the same. . . . [In this situation] the priests, of course, would be in charge of the administration and economy. They would conduct trade and regulate foreign relations. In short, they would be responsible for the welfare of the community and would mediate with the divinity on behalf of the people.[43]

Such a system was not without precedent in the Bronze Age. In Mesopotamia, the Sumerians, who created the first advanced civilization in the Tigris-Euphrates valley, had a similar arrangement. The Sumerian priests controlled the local economy, and the temples featured workshops, and storage areas, and acted as redistribution centers for goods. It is possible that when the Minoans were fashioning their own system they were strongly influenced by the Sumerian model.

Looking at the Knossos palace-center as a great temple, one can readily see a reason for the seemingly mazelike nature of the many winding corridors, split levels, and rooms diverging in all directions. It could well be that the architects intended the complexity of the place, as one scholar puts it, "to produce an effect that was bewildering, impressive, and disorienting . . . to create a narrative experience for the [religious] pilgrim . . . an experience full of unsettling incident and surprise."[44] In this scenario, the palace-center was itself a part of the religious experience.

Presumably, those who entered the palace-center to worship stopped at one or more of the many individual shrines located at strategic points in the structure. The Dartmouth team gives this helpful description of one of them. A kind of shrine known as a bench sanctuary (because of its benchlike component), it is located in the southeast section of the Knossos complex.

This tiny (5 ft. x 5 ft.) shrine was abandoned with its religious furniture *in situ* [in their original positions] and is thus extremely valuable as a source for our understanding of Minoan religion. . . . The room's floor area is divided into three sections at different levels. In the front (lowest) part lie several large vases. In the middle area, a tripod "table of offerings" is embedded in the floor, and to either side of it are groups of small jugs and cups. At the back of the room is a raised bench [about two feet high] on which are fixed two . . . clay "horns of consecration." . . . Between the two pairs of "horns" were found a bell-shaped female figurine and a smaller female statuette . . . perhaps a treasured heirloom. To the left of the left-hand pair of "horns" was a male figurine holding out a dove, while to the right of the right-hand pair were two more bell-shaped female figurines, one with a bird perched on her head.[45]

Minoan Deities

Scholars think that the female with the bird on her head depicted in the bench sanctuary was a goddess. At first glance, it would appear that the Minoans were polytheistic, meaning that they worshipped multiple gods.

And this may indeed be the case. However, a number of pieces of evidence suggest that most of these deities may have been seen as different manifestations of the same divinity. This was (in ancient times) and remains quite common in many religions. The classical Greeks worshipped numerous different manifestations of the god Zeus and goddess Athena, for example, each having distinctive attributes. Similarly, many Christians think of the Father, Son, and Holy Ghost as being distinct in one sense yet also as parts of the same divine being.

If this interpretation is correct, the overall Minoan divinity seems to have been a goddess named Potnia, or "the Lady." The Minoans did worship a universal mother-goddess by that name, dedicating numerous shrines to her and mentioning her often in the palace tablets and other inscriptions. One plausible theory is that in the Stone Age and later Pre-Palace eras, the Minoans had multiple deities, mostly female ones; but over time they came to see them as varying manifestations of the mysterious, powerful, and loving Potnia.

One of these sides of Potnia's character (or, alternatively, a separate deity) was a snake goddess. Some evidence suggests that this deity, thought to protect the household, may have later evolved into the goddess Athena of classical times. Another female divinity widely venerated by the Minoans was the "Mistress of the Animals," Britomartis. A number of scholars think that she is the basis for the classical goddess Artemis, also a mistress of animals. There was also a Minoan goddess

A Minoan figurine depicts the snake goddess, who may have been a manifestation of Crete's leading divinity, Potnia.

of vegetation who may have been a manifestation of Potnia.

Male deities were rarer and less important in the Minoan religion. In art, they generally appear as consorts (attendants) to or helpers of the female divinities. In a sense, the male gods were expendable—they could die—but the goddesses were eternal. To emphasize nature's cycles of death and rebirth, each year the male consorts were seen to die and then, aided by the goddesses, miraculously to rise again. An exception was the strong male god Poteidan (or Potidas). Scholars believe he was a Minoan version of Poseidon, originally a

Mycenaean god and later the ruler of the seas to the classical Greeks. It appears that his worship in Crete began with the Mycenaean subjugation of the island.

Religious Symbols and Sacred Animals

These gods all had symbols and often sacred animals associated with them. And some of these became the chief symbols of the Minoan religion. Potnia's main symbols, for instance, were the double ax, the pillar, and the snake. Appropriately, by the opening of the Middle Minoan Period, when the palace-centers began to rise, the double ax

A modern drawing shows two men in the chamber known as the Hall of the Double Axes, at Knossos. The double ax was a major Minoan religious symbol.

was the main Minoan religious symbol, its image seen nearly everywhere. Exactly why the ax evolved as a religious sign is uncertain; but it was likely connected to its use in slaughtering sacrificial animals. It is also significant that the word for the double ax was *labrys*. The word *Labyrinth*, denoting the maze of the Theseus legend, likely derived from the term *labyrinthos*, meaning "house of the double ax."

Another sacred symbol, the pillar, manifested itself in a number of ways. It almost certainly originated with the large stalagmites that served as centerpieces of worship in the cave sanctuaries. Later, pillars, either as structural components or free standing, became major features of the palace-centers.

Of the animals sacred to the Minoans, the snake, often seen crawling from holes in the ground, was appropriately a symbol of earth goddesses. Birds were seen as manifestations of divinities who dwelled on mountaintops or in the sky. Especially important was the bull, whose horns of consecration were major themes in Minoan paintings, architecture, and figurines. Cattle and bulls were routinely killed and eaten in sacrifices, and bulls were used in special religious rituals in or near the palaces.

Religious Rituals and Ceremonies

The most famous of these bull rituals were those in which young Minoan men and women allegedly met these creatures head on and vaulted over their backs. The renowned Bull Leaping Fresco, found in the east wing of the Knossos palace, shows three stages of this acrobatic feat. On the far left, a young woman grasps the creature's horns in preparation for the vault; in the middle, a young man somersaults over the bull's back;

and on the right, a young woman lands gracefully on her feet, like a modern gymnast recovering from the high bar. Similar scenes appear on surviving Minoan seals.

Generally speaking, modern scholars are somewhat divided about these depictions of Minoan bull leaping. Some think that no such leaps actually happened and view them as fabrications meant to convey some kind of mystical idea or to illustrate mythical characters and events. Many other experts do accept that such leaps occurred but are unsure what their significance was. Perhaps the confrontation between the vaulters and the sacred beast was meant to emphasize some crucial connection between humanity and the divine. Scholars also differ on where these feats took place. Some think they were staged in the open courtyards in the palace-centers; others suggest they took place in special arenas located just outside the palaces.

Whatever its meaning, bull leaping was only one of many rituals and ceremonies of Minoan religion. And like bull leaping, the others are still largely shrouded in mystery. However, scholars have made a number of educated guesses about certain aspects of these rituals. First, it appears that priestesses usually led them. Paralleling the depictions of goddesses and their male consorts, male priests are shown in art as fewer in number and less important than priestesses. Interestingly, the priests are sometimes shown wearing women's clothes; this suggests that they were transvestites (cross-dressers) and/or eunuchs (castrated males), the latter being a common feature of several ancient Eastern religions.

As for the actual ceremonies, the sacrifice (killing and butchering) of cattle and other animals was often involved, as the remains of animal bones at most religious sites (the peak sanctuaries being an exception) attest. Also, one or more of the priestesses, and sometimes the priests, too, apparently performed sacred dances. There is evidence that some or all of them, at least in late Minoan times, wore cow and bull masks. A garbled memory of this image is almost certainly the derivation of the later Greek legend of the half-bull, half-human Minotaur. Recall that in one of the Cretan myths, as recorded by the ancient Greek writer Diodorus Siculus, the "upper part of" the Minotaur's "body down as far as the shoulders had the form of a bull, but the rest had the form of a man."[46] This is exactly how someone wearing a bull mask would look.

The height of some religious ceremonies may have been the moment when the high priestess "became"—that is, seemed to be possessed by—the goddess. Evidently, the possessed priestess stood at a distance from the worshippers in a "window of appearance," perhaps an opening covered by a veil or light screen. Whatever the religious meaning of this may have been at the time, the distance and veil were surely ways to keep the worshippers from examining the priestess too closely and thereby casting doubt on whether she was really possessed.

The most famous of all Minoan paintings—the Bull Leaping Fresco—shows three young Minoans in various stages of a somersault over a huge beast.

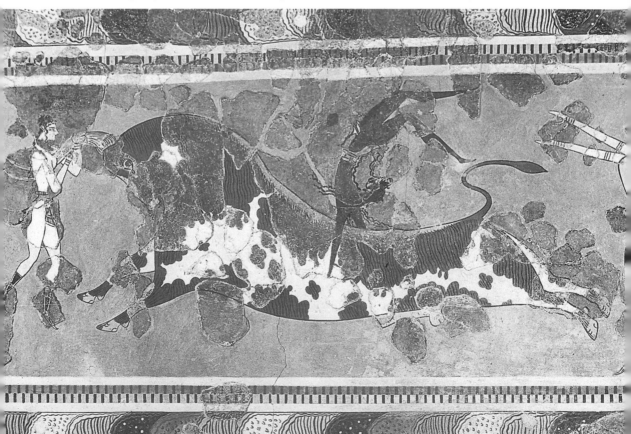

ECHOES OF
MINOAN RELIGION IN MYTHS

Various elements of Minoan religion seem to come together in garbled form in one of the more famous myths about ancient Crete, in which the inventor Daedalus builds the famous Labyrinth for King Minos. These elements include the worship in Crete of the Mycenaean god Poseidon, the sacrifice of bulls, and the fearsome Minotaur, perhaps a distorted memory of Minoan priests wearing bull masks. (This excerpt from the ancient writer Diodorus Siculus's version of the myth was translated by Rhoda A. Hendricks.)

> Because [Daedalus] was admired on account of the skill of his work, he became a friend of Minos, the king. . . . Before this time Minos had customarily dedicated to Poseidon each year the best of the new-born bulls and had sacrificed it to the god. But when there was born an outstandingly fine bull, he sacrificed another bull that was one of the inferior ones. Because Poseidon, as a result, was angry with Minos, he made Minos's wife, Pasiphae, fall in love with the bull and give birth to the Minotaur. . . . They say that . . . the upper part of its body down as far as the shoulders had the form of a bull, but that the rest had the form of a man. It is said that Daedalus built a labyrinth in which this monster could be confined and that it had winding passages that were hard for those who were not used to them to find their way in.

The Sacred Versus the Profane

These facts and suppositions about Minoan religion may make that ancient faith sound rather strange, even completely alien, to modern people. However, it must be kept in mind that religion played a larger role in everyday Minoan life than it does for most people today. Also, the Minoans viewed the world and the concept of the divine rather differently than modern people do. Nanno Marinatos offers these wise and telling parting words:

Economic, religious, and everyday activities must have been intermingled to such an extent, that a distinction between the secular and the religious is irrelevant and artificial. The opposition between the sacred and the profane is a mental construct applicable to our own times and civilization, and attempts to impose it upon this very different culture beclouds our judgment and obstructs our understanding.[47]

71

THE MINOANS AT WAR AND THE MYCENAEAN CONQUEST

One of the major questions raised about the Minoans by archaeologists and historians over the past century is whether that ancient people engaged in warfare. For many decades the traditional view was that the Minoans were peace-loving people who avoided fighting. This pacifistic image seemed to stand in sharp contrast with that of the neighboring Mycenaeans, who were widely viewed as warlike. Among the leading pieces of evidence cited for this scenario was the existence, or lack thereof, of defensive walls. The mainland Mycenaeans built stout ones made of huge stones around their palace-citadels, whereas the Minoan palace-centers on Crete had no defensive walls. Probably, the reasoning went, the Minoans felt they had no need of such walls because their large fleets controlled the Aegean. As for the Mycenaeans, they had either no fleets or none to compare with those of the Minoans. Eventually, according to this view, the Mycenaeans did gain enough strength to invade Crete; and the peace-loving Minoans, having no experience with war, quickly went down to defeat.

This picture of a peaceful race of Minoans who were incapable of defending themselves has increasingly come under fire in recent years. Abundant evidence of Minoan weapons has been found, along with some defensive walls. Also, new interpretations of the layout of the palace-centers suggest that they were not defenseless. Louise Hitchcock writes:

> Today, new discoveries, careful consideration of the existing evidence, and improved methods of analysis are giving scholars new insights into the function of the Minoan palaces. These current findings call into question the popular stereotypes of the so-called "peace-loving" Minoans and "warlike" Mycenaeans. Recent research has determined that the Minoans did, in fact, build walls, and evidence for them has been found at Mallia, Gournia, and at Petras.[48]

The idea that the Minoans did have military capabilities sheds new light on their relationship with the Mycenaeans on the Greek mainland. The evidence shows conclusively that the Mycenaeans eventually conquered Crete. Yet could this have been retaliation or retribution for earlier Minoan military threats or expeditions against the mainland? Were the Minoans the original aggressors in the relationship between the

MINOAN CHARIOTS

It is certain that the Minoans utilized war chariots. Ideograms (written symbols in the form of pictures) for chariots have been found in the Linear B tablets at Knossos and elsewhere. The vehicles thus depicted were very similar in shape and features to a Mycenaean version in a fresco unearthed at Pylos, on the mainland. The chariot's body was made of lightweight wooden slats, and the sides were fashioned of wicker or layers of ox hide stretched across a wooden framework. It had two wheels, each with four spokes, and was pulled by two ponies. It is still unclear exactly how these chariots were used. Most scholars think they were used mainly as "prestige vehicles" to carry important warriors to the battlefield, where they dismounted and fought on foot, although fights between individual pairs of mounted charioteers may have taken place, too.

Evidence shows that the Minoans used chariots similar to the one depicted in this fresco.

two peoples? The image of militarily capable Minoans also raises the question of whether the Minoan city-states fought among themselves. Before these questions can be addressed, however, it is necessary to examine the evidence of Minoan weapons and military traditions and capabilities.

Mythical References to Cretan Militarism

Although a majority of scholars working during the early years of the twentieth century believed the Bronze Age Cretans did not engage in warfare, the classical Greeks were never so misled. A number of myths, which the Greeks accepted as true or at least credible, established that during the Age of Heroes the rulers of Crete possessed strong military forces. Furthermore, these rulers did not hesitate to use these forces. The fifth-century B.C. Greek historian Herodotus wrote that King Minos "had great military success and extended his conquests over a wide area."[49]

More specifically, Herodotus claimed that the Cretans sent an invasion force to the island of Sicily, then called Sicania, lying at the foot of the Italian boot:

Some of the walls built at the ancient Cretan town of Gournia, pictured here, may have been used for defense, although not all scholars are convinced.

Encouraged by omens from heaven, [the Cretans] went with a large fleet to Sicania, where for five years they besieged [the town of] Camicus. . . . Unable to take the place or to continue the siege because of lack of provisions, they finally gave up and went away. In the course of their voyage they were caught by a violent storm off [the coast of Italy] and driven ashore.[50]

The first-century B.C. Greek geographer Strabo mentioned these same events. And both authors agreed that the shipwrecked Cretans stayed and established new towns on Italian soil. Later, Herodotus said, the Italian city of Tarentum "suffered severe loss in attempting to overthrow"[51] these towns.

He also said that the later Greeks "were indebted to" King Minos and the Cretans for inventing "crests on helmets, putting devices [painted images] on shields, and making shields with handles."[52]

Other ancient writers said that the Bronze Age Cretans engaged in warfare. In the *Iliad*, Homer tells how the Cretans contributed a contingent of fighters to the Greek army that besieged Troy. Leading the Cretans was "the great spearman Idomeneus" and warrior Meriones, who was said to be a match for "the man-destroying war-god [Aries]."[53] There are also Thucydides' assertions that King Minos's fleets attacked and destroyed gangs of pirates in the Aegean region.

All of these legendary stories suggest that the Cretans, whom we know today as the

CRETAN WARRIORS FIGHT AT TROY

This is part of Homer's description, in his *Iliad* (E.V. Rieu's translation), of the Cretan (perhaps Minoan) warrior Idomeneus in the midst of battle against his Trojan opponents.

Idomeneus, though he was no longer a young man, flung himself into the fight with a shout to his troops. He struck panic into the Trojans by killing Othryoneus, an ally [of theirs]. . . . Idomeneus let fly at him with a glittering spear and caught him as he swaggered along. The bronze cuirass [chest protector] that he was wearing served him ill. The spear-point landed in the middle of his belly, and he fell to earth with a crash. Idomeneus mocked him . . . [and then] seized him by the foot and began to drag him through the crowd. But now [the Trojan] Asius came to the rescue. He was on foot in front of his chariot. . . . Asius did his utmost to dispatch Idomeneus. But Idomeneus was too quick for him. He hit him with a spear on the throat, under the chin, and the point went right through. Asius fell like an oak . . . that woodmen cut down in the mountains.

Minoans, had weapons and were aggressive, militarily strong, and effective fighters. Granted, one must be careful not to take such myths too literally, as they probably contain a certain amount of exaggeration and fabrication. Yet it has been shown that other myths about Bronze Age Crete (the Labyrinth, Minotaur, bull sacrifices, and so forth) had a basis in fact; and there is no pressing reason to doubt that these, too, were based on memories of real incidents passed down through the filter of centuries of oral retellings.

Armor and Weapons

Moreover, some recent archaeological discoveries do back up some of the elements of these myths. Herodotus's mention of Cretan helmets and shields was confirmed when remnants of both, as well as artistic representations of them, were found in the ruins of Knossos and other Minoan sites. The helmets included bronze versions with mountings for horsehair plumes exactly like those described by Herodotus. Moreover, Homer mentioned that the Cretans and other Greeks who fought at Troy also wore helmets made from boar tusks. Just such a boar-tusk helmet was discovered in a Minoan grave at Knossos.

Herodotus was not alone among the later Greeks to describe highly distinctive Bronze Age Cretan shields. In the *Iliad*, the Cretan leader Idomeneus is in the midst of a savage battle when a Trojan soldier hurls a spear at him. "Idomeneus was looking out," Homer writes,

and avoided the bronze spear by sheltering behind the rounded shield he always carried. It was built of con-

centric rings of oxhide and . . . wa[s] fitted with a couple of crossbars. H[e] crouched under cover of this and th[e] bronze spear flew over him.[54]

Excavations at Knossos and elsewher[e] Crete have brought to light paintings carvings depicting Minoan shields sha[ped] like figure eights, with two circular sect[ions] These were covered with ox hide and fitted with handles on wooden cross[...] specific elements mentioned by Home[r] Herodotus.

The Minoans also had swords and da[ggers] as well as war chariots. A number of sw[ords] have been recovered by archaeologist[s] cluding a handsome one with a matc[hing] dagger found at Mallia. One of the fine[st] all the surviving Minoan swords, fou[nd] Knossos, has a gold-plated handle deco[rated] with a carved scene of a lion killing a [...] Meanwhile, the Knossos tablets featu[re] ages of war chariots. These lightwe[ight] wooden vehicles were likely introduc[ed] the Minoans by the Egyptians, who ad[opted] them from a Near Eastern people (the [Hyk]sos) during the mid-second millennium[...]

Inter-Minoan Warfare?

Having established that the Minoan[s] possess lethal weapons and were not a[verse] to using them, it is natural to wonder [if] Cretan city-states fought one another. A[s] been pointed out, the general consens[us] scholars used to be that Minoan Cret[e] largely a peaceful place where everyon[e] along. Yet is this realistic? It is well d[ocu]mented that the Cretan city-states o[f] classical era warred almost constantly territory and other matters. And the cla[ssical] Greek mainland states incessantly squa[bbled]

This colorful series of figures accurately depicts the armor and weapons wielded by Bronze Age Mycenaean and Minoan warriors.

as well. So it would be truly remarkable if several Minoan states, each rich in human and material resources, existed beside one another for more than five centuries without ever going to war.

This does not mean that such a long period of peace among the Bronze Age Cretans is impossible. As Maitland Edey suggests:

> It can be argued that the Minoans did not fight among themselves because . . . it was in the mutual interest of all not to do so. This mutuality could have been based on some sort of island-wide network of religious control and/or economic interdependence.

. . . The redistributive system itself, in its developed palace form, could have been a deterrent to warfare.[55]

However, as Edey admits, it is just as likely that the Minoans did fight one another from time to time. That no solid archaeological evidence for such fighting has yet been found is hardly surprising. A number of battlefields from Greece's later Classical Age have disappeared from view; and most of those whose locations have been firmly identified have changed so much over the centuries that they show few or no signs of human strife.

There is also the distinct possibility that the Minoans did not generally fight battles in the conventional manner—pitting hundreds or thousands of soldiers against one another in huge melees. In Homer's *Iliad*, major warriors sometimes fight one-on-one while their respective armies watch. Other examples of such formal, prearranged individual fights deciding the outcome of disputes are known from various ancient societies. Perhaps the Minoans, who appear to have been extremely pious in all aspects of their lives, had religious codes that allowed, or even demanded, that arguments be settled this way. Such small-scale battles would leave no trace in the archaeological record.

The Rise of the Mycenaeans

How and how often the Cretan city-states fought one another ultimately proved less crucial to their well-being than their fateful military confrontation with the Mycenaeans. Before exploring that event (or series of events), it is necessary first to consider who the Mycenaeans were and the nature of their long-standing relationship with the Minoans. Scholars differ somewhat about when the first Mycenaeans arrived in Greece. But the most likely scenario is that in about 2000 B.C. they began migrating in waves into the Greek peninsula, from the north or northeast or both. These newcomers then either overcame or mingled with the native inhabitants, who had been around since the Stone Age.

During their early centuries on the mainland, the Mycenaeans must have stood in awe of the Minoans, whose magnificent

The interiors of the Mycenaean palaces were similar to, although smaller in scale, than those in Crete. This cutaway drawing reconstructs the palace at Pylos on the mainland.

palace-centers and large fleets controlled the whole Aegean sphere. At the same time that the Minoans were creating exquisite wall frescoes, enjoying the benefits of indoor plumbing, and trading with faraway Egypt, the Mycenaeans were largely impoverished shepherds and farmers living in small, culturally backward villages. It is only natural, therefore, that as they rose from their backward state the Mycenaeans were strongly influenced by their island neighbors. Over time, the mainlanders borrowed styles of dress, artistic motifs, and other cultural aspects from the Minoans.

Eventually (probably sometime between 1650 and 1500 B.C.), the Mycenaeans established small kingdoms in the southern reaches of the Greek mainland. The strongest of these were centered at Mycenae and Tiryns, both in the northeastern Peloponnesus; Pylos on the southwestern coast of that peninsula; Athens, lying to the northeast on another peninsula (Attica); and Thebes in Boeotia (pronounced bee-OH-shya), the region just north of Attica. The rulers of each kingdom dwelled in a stone palace-citadel. Though considerably smaller and less sophisticated than the Minoan palace-centers, these mainland fortresses had more formidable defenses.

Minoan Domination of the Mainlanders?

An important question is why the Mycenaeans felt the need to fortify themselves to such a degree. On the one hand, it can be reasonably argued that the mainland kings fought among themselves over territory and other grievances. It is also quite probable that the Mycenaeans wanted to protect themselves from the Minoans. After all, the

latter did possess a powerful fleet of ships as well as plenty of metal swords and other offensive weapons. And some evidence suggests that the islanders tried to exert some kind of political or even military control over the mainlanders. In his biography of Theseus, for example, Plutarch briefly mentions an ancient tradition that King Minos carried on "a war of devastation against the Athenians,"[56] who in the Bronze Age were Mycenaeans.

Some scholars go further and contend that the mainland citadels were, for some undetermined time span, tributary states in a larger Minoan empire. Tribute is money or valuables paid by one party to acknowledge the dominance of another; so a tributary state is one that generally does the bidding of a stronger one and pays the stronger one what amounts to protection money to avoid punishment or subjugation. Noted historian J.D.S. Pendlebury and others have argued that this is exactly the kind of political situation reflected in the famous myth of Theseus. Recall that in the story, Athens, a mainland Mycenaean state, is forced to turn over to the ruler of Knossos a group of young men and women every nine years. This sounds as if the Minoans at Knossos periodically took hostages in order to ensure Athens's good behavior. These hostages were specifically referred to as "tribute" by Plutarch and other ancient writers who recorded the story.

There is another piece of relevant textual evidence from the Theseus story that is often overlooked by scholars. It not only reveals Minoan political domination over the Mycenaeans but also explains why the latter increasingly felt compelled to fight their oppressors. "There was," Plutarch writes "a decree in force throughout Greece that no

Paintings from Greek vases of the Classical period show the legendary Athenian leader Theseus and his troops. He may have been a real person.

trireme [warship] should sail from any port carrying a crew of more than five men."[57] The use of the word *decree* is telling. The issuing and enforcing of a decree presupposes that the party doing the issuing and enforcing has some sort of control over the party that receives that command. Here, it seems probable that the ruler (or rulers) of Crete maintained their naval superiority and control of the Aegean by forbidding the Mycenaeans from building or launching full-fledged fleets of ships. This would also have barred the Mycenaeans from any major participation in the lucrative long-

range trade with Palestine and Egypt that the Minoans enjoyed.

The Mycenaean Conquest

Considering the volatile political situation just described, the Mycenaean rulers had ample motivation to launch military strikes against Crete. This eventually happened, although exactly how remains unknown. According to the legendary account of Theseus's adventures, Athens launched at least one military expedition against the Knossos city-state. The following is Plutarch's version:

When the ships were ready, he set out, taking . . . a number of Cretan exiles as his guides. The Cretans had no warning of his movements . . . so that Theseus was able to seize the harbor, disembark his men, and reach Knossos before his arrival was discovered. There he fought a battle at the gates of the Labyrinth and killed Deucalion [son of the ruler of Knossos] and his bodyguard. As Ariadne [the local ruler's daughter] now succeeded to the throne, he made a truce with her, recovered the young Athenians, and concluded a pact of friendship between the Athenians and the Cretans, who swore that they would never in the future begin a war with Athens.[58]

Again, such mythical accounts must not be viewed as historical documents to be taken literally. Some of the names and events described may be fabricated or they may conflate (combine) people and events from different times and places. Yet the general thrust of this story—that during the second millennium B.C., Greek mainlanders

This lavish reconstruction of Mycenaean warriors preparing for battle shows their boar's tusk helmets and ox-hide-covered shields.

attacked and defeated the Cretans at Knossos —has been absolutely confirmed by the archaeological record. Sometime during the 1400s B.C., the forces of one or more Mycenaean kingdoms invaded Crete and took over Knossos and the other Minoan palace-centers; this is shown by widespread evidence that the palaces were burned and by physical and artistic evidence showing that Mycenaeans were subsequently in charge.

This did not by any means mark the end of Minoan civilization; the local populations of the Cretan states remained intact and went about their lives. What had changed was that they now had to obey foreign masters. These overlords evidently ruled the whole island from Knossos, which was partly or largely rebuilt over the next few years. At least from that redistribution center, the collective economy seems to have continued to operate. One difference was that Linear B, the Mycenaean script, largely replaced Linear A, the older Minoan script, for palace record keeping. Another difference was that in post-invasion Crete, with most of the old palace-centers now in ruins, many of the towns and villages far from Knossos had to become more self-sustaining. At the same time, as the archaeological evidence shows, many Minoans turned away from the sea, abandoning villages near the coasts and building new ones farther inland.

The burning question for the scholars who originally pieced together this invasion scenario was: Why were the Mycenaeans so successful? They lacked large fleets and had long been far less organized and powerful than the Minoans. Yet they were suddenly able to sweep aside the mighty Minoan navy and defeat all of the Cretan city-states. Some scholars wondered if something might have happened to the Minoans to weaken them and make them more vulnerable to conquest. This turned out indeed to be the case. And quite unexpectedly, archaeologists discovered the agent of the Minoans' decline on a tiny island lying not far north of Crete.

CHAPTER SEVEN

MINOAN CIVILIZATION IS CRIPPLED BY A VOLCANIC ERUPTION

Spyridon Marinatos was thirty-one in 1932, when, as a young Greek archaeologist, he made a discovery that was destined to lead to important new revelations about the Minoans and the decline of their splendid civilization. For years, he had been intrigued by the excavations of Minoan sites at Knossos, Phaistos, and Mallia. At the time, these digs were still ongoing and yielding a stream of new information about the enigmatic Minoans. Meanwhile, previously unknown Minoan villages and houses were coming to light all across Crete. Certain that many more lay buried, awaiting the spades of archaeologists to free them from the silent earth, Marinatos was determined to find them.

To aid in his quest, the young excavator turned to the works of the ancient writers, much as Heinrich Schliemann had done in his own search for Troy. Something mentioned by Homer, and later by Strabo, caught Marinatos's eye. Both authors said that Knossos, situated a couple of miles inland from Crete's northern coast, had had a harbor town at Amnisos. Following this clue Marinatos went to Amnisos, and it did not take him long to strike pay dirt. He soon discovered two Minoan country mansions, one featuring the remains of some beautiful frescoes of lilies and other plants. Appropriately, the structure became known as the Villa of the Frescoes.

While he was working at the Amnisos site, two peculiar finds captured Marinatos's attention. First, the other villa was filled with pumice, a light, porous material emitted by volcanoes. Second, some of the walls of the villas had fallen in an odd manner; it appeared that the huge, heavy stone blocks had been pulled outward and thrown many yards away, which would not have occurred in an earthquake. "What really piqued [stimulated] my interest," Marinatos later wrote, "were the curious positions of several huge stone blocks that had been torn from their foundations and strewn around the sea."[59] The young scholar reasoned that the only force strong enough to account for what he had found was one or more giant sea waves, today called tsunamis.

The discovery of volcanic debris and evidence of tsunami damage at Amnisos made Marinatos think about the tiny island of Thera, lying almost directly north of Amnisos and Knossos. Geologists had already confirmed that the volcano on that island had erupted violently sometime during the mid-second millennium B.C. The more Marinatos thought about it, the more he

MODERN THERA: AN AWESOME SIGHT

The devastating power of Thera's Bronze Age eruption can still be seen in the topography of the Theran island group, which is composed of three parts. The main island in the group (called Thera) is shaped like a narrow crescent. The curving ends of the crescent partly enclose a nearly circular bay about six miles in diameter, while the two other islands (Therasia and tiny Aspronisi) lie on the far side of the bay. Sailing into the bay, one immediately encounters an awesome sight. The inner side of Thera's crescent is made up of sheer cliffs that tower to a height of 1,200 feet in some places. And a layer of volcanic ash and pumice from 60 to 150 feet deep rests on top of the cliffs (and lies beneath the soil across the whole island). Meanwhile, in the middle of the bay, the volcano, which has undergone several smaller eruptions in the past three thousand years, has broken the surface and has begun to make new islands. A few thousand years from now, a new volcanic cone will tower over Thera, and the destructive cycle will repeat itself.

A large cruise ship is dwarfed by the towering cliffs that make up the rim of Thera's enormous bay (a volcanic caldera).

suspected that the eruption had struck the Minoans a tremendous blow, perhaps one from which they were ultimately unable to recover.

Today, it is clear that Marinatos was essentially correct about the devastating effects of the Bronze Age eruption. Both geologic and archaeological evidence shows that sometime between about 1625 and 1500 B.C. the Theran volcano exploded violently enough to rank the event as the worst natural disaster in recorded history. The eruption caused huge tsunamis that devastated the surrounding islands, including Crete. And the effects of the catastrophe were felt as far away as Palestine and Egypt. The general consensus of scholars is that the Minoans did manage to survive the disaster; however, it weakened and disoriented them enough that they were unable to resist the onslaught of the Mycenaeans, who capitalized on the islanders' misfortunes. Moreover, studies of the Theran eruption and its devastation of the Minoan sphere have generated a fascinating corollary theory. Many scholars are convinced that folk memories of that great disaster gave rise to the myth of the sinking of Atlantis, the so-called lost continent.

The Discovery of Akrotiri

Marinatos published an account of his findings at Amnisos in the scholarly journal *Antiquity* in 1939. This marked the first time that an archaeologist had suggested that a volcano had crippled Minoan Crete, and a number of scholars remained skeptical. They agreed that the Theran volcano had erupted in Minoan times. But in their view the evidence Marinatos had found at Amnisos, though intriguing, was by itself not

enough to prove the eruption had disastrously affected all of Crete. Marinatos was eager to find other evidence to support his thesis. In particular, he wanted to search for Minoan towns on Thera. But World War II and then a Greek civil war intervened, bringing archaeological work in Greece almost to a halt.

As a result of these and other circumstances, Marinatos was not able to begin excavations on the island of Thera until 1967. By that time, he was Greece's leading archaeologist and was recognized as one of the world's foremost experts on the Greek Bronze Age. As his boat entered Thera's central bay, he could not help but envision the bay's formation in the great Bronze Age eruption. The main section of Thera is shaped like a narrow crescent, with its curving arms partially enclosing the bay, which is about six miles in diameter. The inner side of the island's crescent is composed of a series of towering cliffs that rise as high as twelve hundred feet from the water's surface.

Marinatos was well aware that before the great disaster of the second millennium B.C. neither these cliffs nor the bay itself had existed. Thera had been a roughly circular island with a massive volcano located near its center. In the early stages of the eruption, the volcano had spewed out immense quantities of ash, pumice, and other debris, some of which, Marinatos realized, he had discovered at Amnisos. These early stages of the eruption steadily emptied the huge magma chamber beneath the volcano. (Magma is hot molten rock that sometimes rises to Earth's surface.)

For many thousands of years, the magma within the chamber had supported the heavy volcanic cone (or cones) above. But

Avant l'éruption de 1866

En Mars 1866

En Mai 1866

These drawings, dating from 1866, show that year's small eruption of the Theran volcano. The eruption of ca. 1625–1500 B.C. devastated the Minoans.

when this monstrous cavern emptied, gravity inevitably took over and a large section of the island suddenly collapsed, forming a deep circular depression called a caldera. Marinatos marveled that the sheer cliffs that towered above him were the upper sections of the caldera's walls, which extended deep beneath the waves as well. He tried to place himself back in the Bronze Age and to visualize enormous amounts of seawater rushing in to fill the void created by the collapse. The inrushing water suddenly rebounded and sped outward in all directions. Some of the tsunamis thus created came ashore on the northern coast of Crete and smashed into the buildings at Amnisos, dislodging the large stones that Marinatos had found there. In fact, the waves had struck all of Crete's coasts, often rushing far inland and destroying entire towns.

Though fascinated by this scenario of natural destruction, Marinatos had not journeyed to Thera merely to study the physical effects of the great eruption. He was convinced that Thera had been an important Minoan colony or ally, perhaps even linked closely by politics and/or religion to the Knossos city-state. If he could find a major Minoan town buried beneath the layers of volcanic ash on Thera, it would prove that the eruption had damaged the Minoans on a wide scale.

Marinatos found what he was looking for near Akrotiri, a small village on Thera's southern coast. Slowly but steadily, the shovels of his team of workers began unearthing the remains of a Bronze Age Minoan city dating to the middle of the second millennium B.C. Tragically, Marinatos died in 1974 from injuries sustained when he fell from an ancient wall excavated at Akrotiri. But the archaeologists who succeeded him continued the work he had initiated there. To date, excavators have found several ancient streets filled with residences and shops, some of them two stories high. Numerous storage jars and other artifacts, as well as a number of magnificent frescoes, have also been unearthed. Only a small portion of the original town has been uncovered so far. Archaeologists are fairly certain that some of the town disappeared into the caldera when the volcano collapsed, and what remains will likely take at least several more decades to excavate and properly study.

Myths as Memories

The discovery of a Minoan town buried and well preserved by layers of volcanic ash on Thera, coupled with eruption damage on Crete, showed that the Bronze Age eruption did significant damage to the Minoans. But how significant? Was the disaster large and severe enough to have disrupted the Minoans' trading empire and entire way of life?

As this photo shows, some of the two-story houses at Akrotiri, the Theran town buried by the great Bronze Age eruption, are still partially intact.

As always, supplementing the archaeological evidence are scattered but very telling pieces of literary evidence. A number of scholars have remarked that it would be surprising if the memory of a catastrophe so huge was not preserved in surviving folklore and writings in Greece and other nearby regions. And this appears to be exactly what happened. The Greek epic poet Hesiod, who lived during the late eighth century B.C., retold a myth familiar to the classical Greeks in which the god Zeus battled with a giant monster. "The whole earth boiled and heaven and the sea," Hesiod wrote. "The great waves raged along the shore . . . and endless quakes arose. Great Earth groaned."[60] The earthquakes, giant waves, and loud roar here described could well be dim and somewhat distorted memories of the formation of Thera's caldera and its deadly aftereffects.

Other memories of the same disaster seem to have been preserved in a legend set to paper by the fifth-century Athenian playwright Euripides in his *Hippolytus*. A messenger tells the king of Athens:

> There is a stretch of shore that [faces] the Saronic Gulf. Here, from the ground a roar like Zeus's thunderclap came sounding heavy round us, terrible to hear. . . . And when we looked upon the foaming shores, we saw a monstrous wave towering up to the sky. . . . Swelling up and surging onward, with all around [it] a mass of foam . . . it neared the shore.[61]

The Saronic Gulf is located along the southeastern coast of the Greek mainland, facing right in the direction of Thera. A tsunami created by the collapse of Thera's volcano would surely have entered the gulf,

where witnesses along the headland would have seen it and likely been filled with awe and fear. Similar legends of great waves and floods abound in the folklore of ancient peoples living along the coasts of the Aegean and eastern Mediterranean.

Even faraway Egypt produced legends and writings that appear to be linked to the Bronze Age Theran catastrophe. This is not surprising since the Theran tsunamis, although much reduced in size after their long journey, had to have struck Egypt's northern coast. Moreover, the airborne ash from the eruption would have caused the sky to grow dark across much of the eastern Mediterranean basin. An inscription by the pharaoh Ahmose (who reigned from 1550 to 1525 B.C.) reads, in part:

> The gods expressed their discontent. . . . A tempest . . . caused darkness in the western region [i.e., the part of Egypt lying closest to the Aegean]. The sky was unleashed . . . more than the roar of the crowd. . . . Houses and shelters [from local villages destroyed by the waves] were floating on the water . . . for days.[62]

The Minoans in a Downward Spiral

If the effects of the eruption were so pronounced in Egypt, which lies hundreds of miles from Thera, it stands to reason that they were much more severe in Crete, located a mere seventy miles from the epicenter of the disaster. And indeed, archaeologists have found evidence that many square miles of Cretan farmland were covered by layers of ash and were at least temporarily ruined. Other evidence suggests

The Greek god Zeus battles his enemies in this painting from the late Renaissance. Some such myths may be based on distorted memories of the Theran catastrophe.

that most buildings near the coasts, where a majority of people lived, were badly damaged. Also, it is almost certain that most of the Minoan merchant vessels and warships were destroyed by the waves. Maitland Edey tells how such devastation likely forced Minoan culture into a downward spiral that weakened it and left it, for the first time in its history, wide open to attack by enemies and opportunists:

> If we . . . concede, as some archaeologists maintain, that damage was

done to the Minoan palaces and towns by a combination of earthquakes and tsunamis stemming from the blast on Thera; if we assume that most . . . of Crete's ships were swamped in the harbors around the island, crippling her defenses and reducing her ability to trade overseas; if we assume that the agricultural basis of the country's economy was jolted by a disastrous ash-fall that blanketed the eastern half of Crete; if, in short, we presume a number of volcanic events on Thera doing one thing or another to start a downward slide in the Minoan economy, then we begin to see how [Minoan power declined].

Edey hastens to add that, despite the ravages of nature described, "the actual destruction of the palaces . . . on Crete was the work not of volcanoes but of men."[63] These "men" were, of course, the mainland Mycenaeans. Probably in stages, over the course of a few decades during the 1400s B.C., the invaders took advantage of the Minoans' plight and seized control of the major palace-centers in Crete.

The change from a Minoan regime to a Mycenaean one was well known to and documented by the Egyptians, who now found Mycenaean traders, rather than Minoan ones, arriving on their shores. During the crucial century in question, the costumes of the Keftiu depicted in Egyptian tombs underwent a change in style. Archaeologists found that the Minoan-style cutaway kilts had been purposely painted over to show wraparound kilts, the style more commonly worn by the mainland Mycenaeans. Scholar J.V. Luce points out, "The change in this tomb decoration can hardly be discounted as a mere artistic whim. It must surely have po-

MARINATOS COMPARES THERA TO KRAKATOA

In formulating his theory that an eruption of the Theran volcano devastated Minoan Crete, Spyridon Marinatos looked closely at a similar caldera-forming volcanic event that had occurred more recently. In 1883 the volcano on the island of Krakatoa, in Indonesia, had collapsed and generated large tsunamis. Drawing parallels between the two eruptions, he wrote in his 1939 article for the journal *Antiquity*:

> The island of Krakatoa is much smaller than Thera and the part of it that was submerged was about a quarter of the other (22.8 square km against 83 in Thera). . . . Vast quantities of pumice coated both the island [of Krakatoa] and a great part of the sea round about. . . . A tremendous roar accompanied the explosion [i.e., the final collapse] and was heard over 2,000 miles away—just one-twelfth of the earth's circumference. . . . But worst of all was a series of terrific waves which rose after the explosion. They were as much as 90 feet high, and broke with devastating force and speed against the coasts of Java and Sumatra. Where they struck a plain, they swept inland, and as far as [3,000 feet] inland they were still [45 feet] high. Whole towns, villages and woods were destroyed. . . . The amazing catastrophe cost over 36,000 lives.

The Theran disaster caused the Minoan economy to decline steadily. Eventually, the palace-centers, including the one at Knossos (pictured), were abandoned.

litical significance. As such, it seems very good evidence for [regime] change at Knossos."[64]

After the Mycenaean invasion, Crete's palace-centered economy must have steadily declined in organization and productivity. After all, most of these centers were burned and never rebuilt. And although the one at Knossos was partially restored, around 1380 B.C. or so it burned again and was then largely abandoned. In the years that followed, the surviving Minoan farmers, herders, and craftspeople may have been compelled to turn over a set proportion of what they produced to Mycenaean collectors; in this scenario, the goods were loaded onto ships and taken to the mainland to enrich the Mycenaean nobility.

Minoan Crete and Lost Atlantis

The Theran eruption changed Minoan society forever because the people who had erected the great palace-centers of Crete were never able to regain control of their island or their destiny. As archaeology shows, however, they went on with their lives and clung to their old traditions and customs. Recall once more Homer's description of Crete's population in the late Bronze Age, which in its post-invasion context takes on new meaning: "Each of the several races of the isle has its own language. First, there are the Achaeans [i.e., the Mycenaeans]; then the genuine Cretans [the Minoans], proud of their native stock."[65]

These last generations of Minoans no doubt passed on accounts of the great natural catastrophe that had devastated their island. And the great volcanic event continued to be remembered in the folklore of the Greeks who inherited the Greek sphere from the Minoans and the Mycenaeans. This is shown in the writings of Hesiod,

ATLANTEAN AND MINOAN BULL HUNTS

Two of the strongest arguments for identifying the Minoans with the Atlanteans are that each used bulls in their temple ceremonies and each captured bulls in precisely the same manner. According to Plato (in Benjamin Jowett's translation of the *Critias*), the Atlanteans "hunted the bulls without weapons but with staves [wooden sticks] and nooses." And after the animals were sacrificed, the kings "filled a bowl of wine and cast in a clot of [bull's] blood for each of them" and then "drew [wine] from the bowl in golden cups." In the early years of the twentieth century, two Minoan golden goblets (known as the Vapheio cups) were discovered. Carved on their sides is a perfectly preserved scene of men hunting bulls with sticks and nooses. Scholar K.T. Frost wrote in 1909:

Plato's words exactly describe the scenes on the famous Vapheio cups, which certainly represent catching wild bulls for the Minoan [bull ritual], which, as we know from the palace itself, differed from all others which the world has seen exactly in the point which Plato emphasizes—namely that no weapons were used.

Some of the bull rituals attributed to the mythical Atlanteans are identical to real rituals performed by the Minoans.

Euripides, and others who mention great earthquakes and sea waves ravaging the Aegean region during the Age of Heroes.

One well-known classical Greek who seems to have passed along a major recollection of the Bronze Age disaster was the fourth-century B.C. Athenian philosopher Plato. In two of his many dialogues, the *Timaeus* and the *Critias*, he tells the legend of the lost island kingdom of Atlantis. The Atlanteans had fought a war with the mainland Athenians, he says, which the Athenians had won. After that, Atlantis sank into the sea in a great natural disaster. For more than two thousand years, the legend of Atlantis has fascinated people around the world and has spawned an immense number of writings, many of them attempting to identify the location of the lost island. Locales ranging from the Atlantic Ocean and the Caribbean Islands, to North Africa, Scandinavia, and Antarctica have been suggested.

In 1909 classical scholar K.T. Frost reviewed recent findings in Crete and saw close parallels between the Minoans and Plato's Atlanteans. "If the account of Atlantis can be compared with the history of Crete and her relationship with Greece and Egypt," he wrote in an article for the *Times* of London,

> it seems almost certain that here we have an echo of the Minoans. . . .

The whole description of Atlantis which is given in the *Timaeus* and the *Critias* has features so thoroughly Minoan that even Plato could not have invented so many unsuspected facts.[66]

Since Frost's day, a number of experts on Greece's Bronze Age have tackled the same issue; and most classical scholars now accept that Plato's Atlantis was a garbled memory of the Minoan civilization on Crete, Thera, and nearby islands. They point to striking similarities between the Atlanteans and the Minoans. In addition to the fact that both fought and lost a war with Athens, both Minoan Crete and Atlantis had a large, fertile plain surrounded by mountains. Also, both worshipped the god Poseidon (clearly a Greek deity); had a large, complex temple where bulls were worshipped; and used identical combinations of sticks and nooses to hunt bulls. Finally, both Atlantis and Crete were struck by a great natural disaster, and Atlantis and most of Minoan Thera sank into the sea in a single day. In a strange twist of fate, therefore, it appears that the long-lost civilization of the Minoans *was* remembered by the classical Greeks and other peoples through the ages, only by a different name. And it took the shovels and creative thinking of modern archaeologists to sort things out.

THE END OF MINOAN-MYCENAEAN CIVILIZATION

In the two centuries following their take-over of Crete, the Mycenaean warlords controlled the Aegean seaways and enjoyed trade with peoples living far beyond. If the legendary Trojan War was a real event (which remains unproven), it occurred toward the end of this period. Perhaps in about 1250 B.C. or somewhat later, an alliance of Mycenaean kings, aided by contingents from Minoan Crete and other Aegean islands the Mycenaeans controlled, sacked Troy, giving rise to the famous legend.

Not long after this event (if indeed it occurred)—in about 1200 B.C. or shortly thereafter—disaster once more struck the Aegean region. That cultural sphere, as well as many parts of the Near East, underwent a period of unexpected and unprecedented upheaval. Most of the major Mycenaean citadels on the mainland suffered sacking and burning and were never rebuilt. Writing, record keeping, large-scale political organization, and other aspects of advanced civilization on the mainland and in Minoan Crete largely disappeared. And Greece slipped into its dark age, which was destined to last for centuries.

Invaders from the North?

The cause or causes of the catastrophe that brought the Minoan-Mycenaean culture in the Aegean sphere to an abrupt end remain uncertain and in some ways a bit mysterious. But scholars have advanced some creative theories to explain the great turmoil. One suggests that civil conflicts among the Mycenaeans led to the sacking of the citadels and a disruption of farming and trade. However, for this to be true, similar civil wars had to have erupted throughout Asia Minor and the Near East at the same time; some experts feel that this is highly unlikely.

In recent years, a different military explanation for the catastrophe of circa 1200 B.C. has been gaining currency among scholars, although it has yet to be universally accepted. Advocates of this theory suggest that large bands of warriors from central Europe swarmed over the lands of the eastern Mediterranean, including Greece and Crete. They point to the appearance of a new type of sword in Greece toward the end of the Bronze Age. A long slashing weapon, it had been developed by tribesmen from central and eastern Europe.

At the same time, according to this view, well-armored foot soldiers of foreign origin appeared in southern Greece. A row of such troops can be seen marching in a painting on the famous Warrior Vase, found at Mycenae. They wear long-sleeved jerkins (some covered with body armor) and horned helmets with upright crests, and carry crescent-shaped shields. Who were these foreign soldiers? The theory in question holds that they were most likely mercenaries (hired troops) recruited from tribes living north of the Mycenaean sphere to aid one or more Mycenaean warlords.

These hired soldiers may well have been impressed by the vast caches of gold and other valuables accumulated by the Mycenaean kings. More importantly, the newcomers quickly realized that their own weaponry and fighting methods were more than a match for those of the people who had hired them. Soldiers returning home spread the word. And soon, large invasion forces descended on the palace-centers of southern Greece. These armies rendered the chariot corps of the Mycenaeans and Minoans obsolete. Vanderbilt University scholar Robert Drews, a chief advocate of this theory for the catastrophe, writes:

> By the beginning of the twelfth century [B.C.] . . . the size of a king's chariotry ceased to make much difference, because by that time chariotry everywhere had become vulnerable to a new kind of infantry. [Such] infantries . . . used weapons and guerilla tactics that were characteristic of bar-

barian hill people but had never been tried en masse in the plains and against the centers of the late Bronze Age kingdoms.[67]

In this scenario, these well-armed northern fighters easily defeated the numerically fewer and militarily less formidable Mycenaean and Minoan foot soldiers. Then they swarmed the chariots, dispatching horses, drivers, and archers alike with javelins and slashing swords. The slaughter left the Mycenaean citadels and their treasures open to plunder and sent the long-lived Mycenaean-Minoan culture into oblivion.

A Dimly Remembered Age

Was this what brought about the final end of the proud, artistically creative, and religiously devout Minoans? For now, no one can say for sure. What is more certain is that the Minoans did not live and labor in vain. From the physical debris, cultural remnants, and disjointed memories of the Age of Heroes arose a new culture in Greece, one that in the fullness of time gave birth to democracy, literature, the theater, and other key elements of Western civilization. Deep in the fabric of modern life, therefore, lay ideas first conceived in the fertile minds of those who, in a dimly remembered age, erected the great palace-center at Knossos.

NOTES

Introduction: The Limitations of the Sources

1. Maitland A. Edey, *Lost World of the Aegean*. New York: Time-Life, 1975, p. 58.
2. Rodney Castleden, *Minoans: Life in Bronze Age Crete*. New York: Routledge, 1993, pp. 160–61.
3. Castleden, *Minoans*, p. 178.

Chapter 1: Arthur Evans and the Discovery of Minoan Civilization

4. Homer, *Odyssey*, trans. E.V. Rieu. Baltimore: Penguin, 1961, p. 292.
5. Plutarch, *Life of Theseus*, in *Parallel Lives*, excerpted in *The Rise and Fall of Athens: Nine Greek Lives by Plutarch*, trans. Ian Scott-Kilvert. New York: Penguin, 1960, p. 22.
6. Richard Ellis, *Imagining Atlantis*. New York: Random House, 1998, pp. 122–23.
7. Arthur Evans, "Knossos: The Palace," *Annual of the British School at Athens*, vol. 6, 1899–1900, pp. 51–52; and quoted in Joan Evans, *Time and Chance: The Story of Arthur Evans and His Forebears*. London: Longmans, Green, 1943, p. 334.
8. Louise A. Hitchcock, "Understanding the Minoan Palaces," *Athena Review*, vol. 3, no. 3, 2003, p. 32.
9. Quoted in Evans, *Time and Chance*, p. 332.
10. Edey, *Lost World of the Aegean*, p. 78.
11. Edey, *Lost World of the Aegean*, p. 84.
12. Evans's dating system is based on changes in pottery styles. Another Minoan dating system is widely used today in conjunction with the traditional one. Proposed by archaeologist Nicolas Platon, it is based on the rise and fall of the palace-centers and breaks down into the Pre-Palace Period (ca. 2600–1900 B.C.), First Palace Period (ca. 1900–1700 B.C.), Second Palace Period (ca. 1700–1380 B.C.,) and Post-Palace Period (ca. 1380–1100 B.C.).
13. Alexandre Farnoux, *Knossos: Searching for the Legendary Palace of King Minos*. New York: Harry N. Abrams, 1993, p. 69.

Chapter 2: Farming, Finances, and Trade in Minoan Crete

14. Thucydides, *The Peloponnesian War*, trans. Rex Warner. New York: Penguin, 1972, p. 37.
15. Thomas R. Martin, *Ancient Greece: From Prehistoric to Hellenistic Times*. New Haven, CT: Yale University Press, 1996, p. 25.
16. Castleden, *Minoans*, p. 46.
17. Castleden, *Minoans*, p. 48.
18. Emily Vermeule, *Greece in the Bronze Age*. Chicago: University of Chicago Press, 1972, p. 148.

19. Castleden, *Minoans*, p. 122.

Chapter 3: Political and Social Life in the Minoan Towns

20. Edey, *Lost World of the Aegean*, p. 66.
21. Castleden, *Minoans*, p. 22.
22. Castleden, *Minoans*, p. 24.
23. Sarah B. Pomeroy et al., *Ancient Greece: A Political, Social, and Cultural History.* New York: Oxford University Press, 1999, p. 14.
24. Pomeroy, *Ancient Greece*, p. 14.
25. Edey, *Lost World of the Aegean*, p. 71.
26. Edey, *Lost World of the Aegean*, p. 71.
27. R.F. Willetts, *The Civilization of Ancient Crete.* New York: Barnes and Noble, 1995, p. 79.
28. Castleden, *Minoans*, p. 7.

Chapter 4: Minoan Painting, Architecture, Crafts, and Writing

29. Pomeroy, *Ancient Greece*, p. 15.
30. Nanno Marinatos, *Art and Religion in Thera: Reconstructing a Bronze Age City.* Athens: D. and I. Mathioulakis, 1984, p. 33.
31. Castleden, *Minoans*, p. 3.
32. Jeremy B. Rutter et al., "Minoan Architecture: The Palaces," *The Prehistoric Archaeology of the Aegean*, Dartmouth College. http://devlab.dartmouth.edu/history/bronze_age.
33. Sylvia L. Horwitz, *The Find of a Lifetime: Sir Arthur Evans and the Discovery of Knossos.* London: Phoenix, 2001, pp. 139–40.
34. Arthur Evans, *The Palace of Minos at Knossos*, vol. 2. London: Macmillan, 1921–1936, pp. 466–67.
35. Evans, "Knossos," pp. 47–48.
36. Jeremy B. Rutter et. al., "Late Minoan Painting and Other Representational Art: Pottery, Frescoes Steatite Vases, Ivories, and Bronzes," *The Prehistoric Archaeology of the Aegean*, Dartmouth College. http://devlab.dartmouth.edu/history/bronze_age.
37. Castleden, *Minoans*, pp. 59.
38. Edey, *Lost World of the Aegean*, p. 31.

Chapter 5: Minoan Religious Places, Gods, and Rituals

39. Jeremy B. Rutter et al., "Minoan Religion," *The Prehistoric Archaeology of the Aegean*, Dartmouth College. http://devlab.dartmouth.edu/history/bronze_age.
40. Castleden, *Minoans*, p. 59.
41. Castleden, *Minoans*, p. 54.
42. Rutter, "Minoan Religion."
43. Marinatos, *Art and Religion in Thera*, p. 26.
44. Castleden, *Minoans*, pp. 150–51.
45. Rutter, "Minoan Religion."
46. Quoted in Rhoda A. Hendricks, ed. and trans., *Classical Gods and Heroes: Myths as Told by the Ancient Authors.* New York: Morrow Quill, 1974, p. 102.
47. Marinatos, *Art and Religion in Thera*, p. 119.

Chapter 6: The Minoans at War and the Mycenaean Conquest

48. Hitchcock, "Understanding the Minoan Palaces," p. 1.
49. Herodotus, *The Histories*, trans. Aubrey de Sélincourt. New York: Penguin, 1972, p. 110.
50. Herodotus, *Histories*, p. 501.
51. Herodotus, *Histories*, p. 501.
52. Herodotus, *Histories*, p. 110.
53. Homer, *Iliad*, trans. E.V. Rieu. Baltimore: Penguin, 1950, p. 57.

54. Homer, *Iliad*, p. 245.
55. Edey, *Lost World of the Aegean*, p. 60.
56. Plutarch, *Life of Theseus*, p. 22.
57. Plutarch, *Life of Theseus*, p. 25.
58. Plutarch, *Life of Theseus*, pp. 25–26.

Chapter 7: Minoan Civilization Is Crippled by a Volcanic Eruption

59. Spyridon Marinatos, "The Volcanic Destruction of Minoan Crete," *Antiquity*, vol. 13, 1939, pp. 429–30.
60. Hesiod, *Theogony*, in *Hesiod and Theognis*, trans. Dorothea Wender. New York: Penguin, 1973, pp. 50–51.
61. Euripides, *Hippolytus*, in *Three Great Plays of Euripides*, trans. Rex Warner. New York: New American Library, 1958, p. 117.

62. Quoted in Rodney Castleden, *Atlantis Destroyed*. New York: Routledge, 1998, pp. 125–26.
63. Edey, *Lost World of the Aegean*, p. 109.
64. J.V. Luce, *Lost Atlantis: New Light on an Old Legend*. New York: McGraw-Hill, 1969, p. 143.
65. Homer, *Odyssey*, p. 292.
66. K.T. Frost, "The Lost Continent," *London Times*, February 9, 1909.

Epilogue: The End of Minoan-Mycenaean Civilization

67. Robert Drews, *The End of the Bronze Age: Changes in Warfare and the Catastrophe ca. 1200 B.C.* Princeton, NJ: Princeton University Press, 1993, p. 97.

CHRONOLOGY

B.C.

ca. 6000

Human habitations first appear in Crete.

ca. 3000–ca. 1100

Greece's Bronze Age, in which people use tools and weapons made of bronze.

ca. 3000

The start of the Early Minoan Period in the Minoan chronology worked out by archaeologist Arthur Evans and his colleagues.

ca. 2200

End of the Early Minoan Period and beginning of the Middle Minoan Period.

ca. 2100

A pictographic writing script appears in Crete.

ca. 2000–1600

Tribal peoples speaking an early form of Greek enter the Greek peninsula from the east or northeast and maybe merge with an indigenous population; their descendants, whom scholars refer to as Mycenaeans, spread across mainland Greece.

ca. 1550

End of the Middle Minoan Period and beginning of the Late Minoan Period.

ca. 1500–ca. 1400

In stages, Mycenaean warlords take over the Minoan palace-centers and major towns of Crete.

ca. 1380

The palace-center at Knossos is burned and largely abandoned. But Minoan-Mycenaean life in the towns and countryside goes on.

ca. 1215?

Mycenaean Greeks sack the trading city of Troy, giving birth to the legend of the Trojan War.

ca. 1200–ca.1100

For reasons still unclear, the Minoan-Mycenaean kingdoms and fortresses suffer widespread destruction and rapidly decline.

ca. 1100

End of the Late Minoan Period.

ca. 1100–800

Greece's Dark Age, in which poverty and illiteracy are widespread and memories of the Minoan-Mycenaean era devolve into myths.

ca. 800–700

The approximate time period in which the Greek bard Homer composes the *Iliad* and the *Odyssey*, epic poems that celebrate the exploits of heroes of the Bronze Age.

ca. 500–323

Greece's Classical Age, in which Greek civilization produces a great burst of high culture.

ca. 355

The Athenian philosopher Plato pens the *Timaeus* and the *Critias*, works that describe the ancient land of Atlantis.

A.D.

1870

Archaeologist Heinrich Schliemann discovers the remains of Troy, initiating modern studies of Greece's Bronze Age cultures.

1900

Arthur Evans begins excavations at Knossos in northern Crete.

1909

Scholar K.T. Frost first draws parallels between Minoan Crete and Plato's Atlantis.

1915

A Minoan palace-center is discovered at Mallia in northern Crete.

1952

Scholar Michael Ventris deciphers Linear B, one of the scripts in use in the Minoan palace-centers, showing it to be an early form of Greek.

1961

A Minoan palace-center is found at Kato Zakro in eastern Crete.

1967
Archaeologist Spyridon Marinatos discovers a Minoan-style Bronze Age city at Akrotiri on the island of Thera (Santorini).

1985
A Minoan palace-center is discovered at Petras in northeastern Crete.

1991
A Minoan palace is discovered at Galatas in north-central Crete.

2004
Excavations continue to unearth and study the remains of a recently discovered large Minoan town, which lies buried beneath the modern Greek city of Khania.

FOR FURTHER READING

Books

Giovanni Caselli, *In Search of Knossos: Quest for the Minotaur's Labyrinth.* New York: Peter Bedrick, 1999. Filled with stunning color photos, this excellent book tells about the discovery and excavation of the leading Minoan palace on Crete.

Peter Connolly, *The Legend of Odysseus.* New York: Oxford University Press, 1986. An excellent, easy-to-read summary of the events of Homer's *Iliad* and *Odyssey*, including many informative sidebars about the way people lived in Mycenaean times.

Deborah N. Lattimore, *The Prince and the Golden Ax.* New York: Harper-Collins, 1988. Aimed at grade school and junior high school students, this colorful fictional account traces the adventures of a Minoan prince in the last days of Minoan civilization.

Don Nardo, *Greenhaven Encyclopedia of Greek and Roman Mythology.* San Diego: Greenhaven, 2002. Contains hundreds of short but informative articles on Greek myths, gods, heroes, and the myth tellers and their works, including the major stories and characters from the Greek Bronze Age.

Sheldon Oberman, *Island of the Minotaur: Tales from Ancient Crete.* Northampton, MA: Interlink, 2003. An excellent compilation of ancient myths relating to the Minoans and Mycenaeans, aimed at grade school readers.

Ian Serraillier, *A Fall from the Sky: The Story of Daedalus.* New York: Walck, 1966. This version of the classic tale of Daedalus and Icarus, who escaped from the Minoan Labyrinth of Knossos on wings of wax, is geared specifically for young readers.

Web Sites

Akrotiri—Lost Atlantis? (www.dragonridge.com/greece/akrotiri.htm). A brief overview of the ancient town of Akrotiri, on the island of Thera, and its connections with the Bronze Age eruption of the island's volcano and possible link to the Atlantis legend. Has some striking photos of the town and surrounding area.

Hellenic Ministry of Culture, "Knossos" (www.culture.gr/2/21/211/ 21123a/ e211wa03.html). Presented by the Greek government, this colorful site provides a useful thumbnail sketch of the great palace that was once the central focus of the Bronze Age Minoan empire. The photos enlarge when clicked.

The Perseus Digital Library, Tufts University Department of the Classics (www.perseus.tufts.edu). The most comprehensive online source about ancient Greece, with hundreds of links to all aspects of Greek history, life, and culture, supported by numerous photos of artifacts.

Works Consulted

Major Works

Rodney Castleden, *Atlantis Destroyed*. New York: Routledge, 1998. An information-packed presentation of the now widely accepted theory that the legend of Atlantis was a garbled memory of the Minoan civilization on the islands of Crete and Thera.

―――, *Minoans: Life in Bronze Age Crete*. New York: Routledge, 1993. A very well researched and useful general synopsis of the Minoans.

Robert Drews, *The Coming of the Greeks: Indo-European Conquests in the Aegean and the Near East*. Princeton, NJ: Princeton University Press, 1988. Discusses the prevailing theories for the settling of mainland Greece and nearby islands before and during the Bronze Age.

Arthur Evans, *The Palace of Minos at Knossos*. 4 vols. London: Macmillan, 1921–1936. The classic work about the Minoans and the palace-center at Knossos by the archaeologist who first excavated the site.

J. Lesley Fitton, *Discovery of the Greek Bronze Age*. London: British Museum, 1995. An excellent summary of modern archaeological discoveries pertaining to Greece's Bronze Age societies.

Charles Freeman, *The Greek Achievement: The Foundation of the Western World*. New York: Viking, 1999. A well-written overview of ancient Greek civilization, touching on cultural endeavors as well as history.

D.A. Hardy, ed., *Thera and the Aegean World III*. 3 vols. London: Thera Foundation, 1990. A collection of essays by noted experts; overall, this is a large, fairly up-to-date, and valuable overview of what scholars know about the Minoans and the Bronze Age eruption of Thera.

Reynold Higgins, *Minoan and Mycenaean Art*. London: Thames and Hudson, 1997. Well researched and authoritative, this is one of the two best sources available on the subject.

Sinclair Hood, *The Minoans: Crete in the Bronze Age*. London: Thames and Hudson, 1971. One of the more insightful and influential scholarly studies of Minoan Crete.

Sylvia L. Horwitz, *The Find of a Lifetime: Sir Arthur Evans and the Discovery of Knossos*. London: Phoenix, 2001. Horwitz provides a good deal of information about the Minoans and their culture while telling the fascinating story of Evans's life and accomplishments.

Nanno Marinatos, *Art and Religion in Thera: Reconstructing a Bronze Age City*. Athens: D. and I. Mathioulakis, 1984. Sound, well-documented commentary from one of the recognized experts on Minoan religion.

———, *Minoan Religion: Ritual, Image, and Symbol*. Columbia: University of South Carolina Press, 1993. A more detailed look by the author at Minoan religious beliefs and practices.

Spyridon Marinatos, *Crete and Mycenae*. London: Thames and Hudson, 1960. A great archaeologist discusses the Minoan and Mycenaean cultures.

———, *Excavations at Thera, 1968–1974*. Athens: Athens Museum, 1975. This summary of Marinatos's excavations at the Theran site of Akrotiri is fascinating reading for anyone interested in ancient history and provides important data about Minoan culture on Thera.

Anna Michalidou, *Knossos: A Complete Guide to the Palace of Minos*. Athens: Ekdotike Athenon, 1993. A useful synopsis of the palace, complemented by several excellent maps and numerous color plates of ruins and frescoes.

Sarah B. Pomeroy et al., *Ancient Greece: A Political, Social, and Cultural History*. New York: Oxford University Press, 1999. A very well organized, detailed, and insightful summary of ancient Greek civilization.

Jeremy B. Rutter et al., "Late Minoan Painting and Other Representational Art: Pottery, Frescoes, Steatite Vases, Ivories, and Bronzes," "Minoan Architecture: The Palaces," and "Minoan Religion," *The Prehistoric Archaeology of the Aegean*, Dartmouth College. http://dev lab.dartmouth.edu/ history/bronze_age. Three among many other up-to-date, informational essays by classical scholar Jeremy Rutter and a team of graduate students and other assistants at Dartmouth College. Highly recommended.

Emily Vermeule, *Greece in the Bronze Age*. Chicago: University of Chicago Press, 1972. One of the classic works about the Greek Bronze Age by a leading scholar.

Other Important Works—Primary Sources

Euripides, *Hippolytus*, in *Three Great Plays of Euripides*. Trans. Rex Warner. New York: New American Library, 1958.

Rhoda A. Hendricks, Ed. and Trans., *Classical Gods and Heroes: Myths as Told by the Ancient Authors*. New York: Morrow Quill, 1974.

Herodotus, *The Histories*. Trans. Aubrey de Sélincourt. New York: Penguin, 1972.

Hesiod, *Theogony*, in *Hesiod and Theognis*. Trans. Dorothea Wender. New York: Penguin, 1975.

Homer, *Iliad*. Trans. E.V. Rieu. Baltimore: Penguin, 1950.

————, *Odyssey*. Trans. E.V. Rieu. Baltimore: Penguin, 1961.

Plato, *Critias* and *Timaeus*, in *The Dialogues of Plato*. Trans. Benjamin Jowett. Chicago: Encyclopaedia Britannica, 1952.

Plutarch, *Parallel Lives*, excerpted in *The Rise and Fall of Athens: Nine Greek Lives by Plutarch*. Trans. Ian Scott-Kilvert. New York: Penguin, 1960.

Thucydides, *The Peloponnesian War*. Trans. Rex Warner. New York: Penguin, 1972.

Modern Sources—Books

L. Sprague de Camp and Catherine C. de Camp, *Ancient Ruins and Archaeology*. Garden City, NY: Doubleday, 1964.

Rhys Carpenter, *Discontinuity in Greek Civilization*. New York: Cambridge University Press, 1966.

John Chadwick, *The Mycenaean World*. New York: Cambridge University Press, 1976.

V.G. Childe, *The Dawn of European Civilization*. London: Routledge and Kegan Paul, 1957.

Oliver Dickinson, *The Aegean Bronze Age*. New York: Cambridge University Press, 1994.

Christos Doumas, *Thera: Pompeii of the Ancient Aegean*. London: Thames and Hudson, 1983.

Robert Drews, *The End of the Bronze Age; Changes in Warfare and the Catastrophe ca. 1200 B.C.* Princeton, NJ: Princeton University Press, 1993.

Maitland A. Edey, *Lost World of the Aegean*. New York: Time-Life, 1975.

Richard Ellis, *Imagining Atlantis*. New York: Random House, 1998.

Joan Evans, *Time and Chance: The Story of Arthur Evans and His Forebears*. London: Longmans, Green, 1943.

Alexandre Farnoux, *Knossos: Searching for the Legendary Palace of King Minos*. New York: Harry N. Abrams, 1993.

Sinclair Hood, *The Home of the Heroes: The Aegean Before the Greeks*. London: Thames and Hudson, 1967.

Pierre Léveque, *The Birth of Greece*. New York: Harry N. Abrams, 1994.

J.V. Luce, *Lost Atlantis: New Light on an Old Legend*. New York: McGraw-Hill, 1969.

J. Alexander MacGillivray, *Minotaur: Sir Arthur Evans and the Archaeology of the Minoan Myth*. New York: Hill and Wang, 2000.

Thomas R. Martin, *Ancient Greece: From Prehistoric to Hellenistic Times.* New Haven, CT: Yale University Press, 1996.

William A. McDonald and Carol G. Thomas, *Progress into the Past: The Rediscovery of Mycenaean Civilization.* Indianapolis: Indiana University Press, 1990.

John Seymour and Herbert Girardet, *Far from Paradise: The Story of Human Impact on the Environment.* Basingstoke, UK: Green, 1986.

William Taylour, *The Mycenaeans.* London: Thames and Hudson, 1983.

Carol G. Thomas and Craig Conant, *Citadel to City-State: The Transformation of Greece, 1200–700 B.C.E.* Indianapolis: Indiana University Press, 1999.

P.M. Warren, "Minoan Crete and Pharaonic Egypt," in *Egypt, the Aegean, and the Levant.* Ed. E.V. Davies. London: British Museum, 1995.

R.F. Willetts, *The Civilization of Ancient Crete.* New York: Barnes and Noble, 1995.

Periodicals

Maria Andreadaki-Vlassiki, "Discoveries at Khania in Western Crete," *Athena Review,* vol. 3, no. 3, 2003.

Jan Driessen, "The Court Compounds of Minoan Crete: Royal Palaces or Ceremonial Centers?" *Athena Review,* vol. 3, no. 3, 2003.

Arthur Evans, "Knossos: The Palace," *Annual of the British School at Athens,* vol. 6, 1899–1900.

K.T. Frost, "The *Critias* and Minoan Crete," *Journal of Hellenic Studies,* vol. 33, 1913.

———, "The Lost Continent," *London Times,* February 9, 1909.

Louise A. Hitchcock, "Understanding the Minoan Palaces," *Athena Review,* vol. 3, no. 3, 2003.

Thomas W. Jacobson, "17,000 Years of Greek Prehistory," *Scientific American,* vol. 234, 1976.

Stuart Manning, "The Bronze Age Eruption of Thera: Absolute Dating, Aegean Chronology, and Mediterranean Cultural Interrelations," *Journal of Mediterranean Archaeology,* vol. 1, 1988.

Spyridon Marinatos, "The Volcanic Destruction of Minoan Crete," *Antiquity,* vol. 13, 1939.

INDEX

PICTURE CREDITS

ABOUT THE AUTHOR

Historian Don Nardo has written or edited numerous volumes about the ancient Greek world, including *Greek and Roman Sport*, *The Age of Pericles*, *The Parthenon*, *Life in Ancient Athens*, *The Decline and Fall of Ancient Greece*, the four-volume *Library of Ancient Greece*, and literary companions to the works of Homer, Euripides, and Sophocles. He resides with his wife, Christine, in Massachusetts.